Mutual Fund Selection

Moshe Levy · Richard Roll

Mutual Fund Selection

From Theory to Practice

Moshe Levy
Hebrew University of Jerusalem
Jerusalem, Israel

Richard Roll
Emeritus, UCLA
Los Angeles, CA, USA

ISBN 978-3-031-69757-9   ISBN 978-3-031-69758-6   (eBook)
https://doi.org/10.1007/978-3-031-69758-6

This Palgrave Macmillan imprint is published by the registered company Springer Nature Switzerland AG
The registered company address is: Gewerbestrasse 11, 6330 Cham, Switzerland

If disposing of this product, please recycle the paper.

To the Pioneers of Financial Economics

CONTENTS

CHAPTER 1

Introduction

Abstract Mutual fund selection is a critical task faced by most investors. This chapter describes the main challenges of mutual fund selection, and lays out the structure of this book, which is aimed at addressing these challenges.

Keywords Mutual funds · Active investing · Exchange traded funds · Sharpe ratio · Alpha · Estimation error

Mutual funds are very useful investment tools: they offer investors a simple way to achieve portfolio diversification. "Active" mutual funds also offer the services of stock selection and market timing. Mutual funds today play a prominent role in capital markets. According to the 2023 Investment Company Institute (ICI) Factbook, 55% of U.S. households invest in mutual funds. This figure is similar to the percentage of households who participate in the equity market (Bogan, 2008), implying that almost all investors investing in stocks do so, at least in part, via investment in mutual funds. This suggests that the selection of mutual fund/s is one of the most important economic decisions for investors.

In 1940, there were only 68 mutual funds in the U.S. market. This number has increased to 7393 by the end of 2022 (see Fig. 1.1). Thus, today there are more mutual funds than individual U.S. stocks. The main

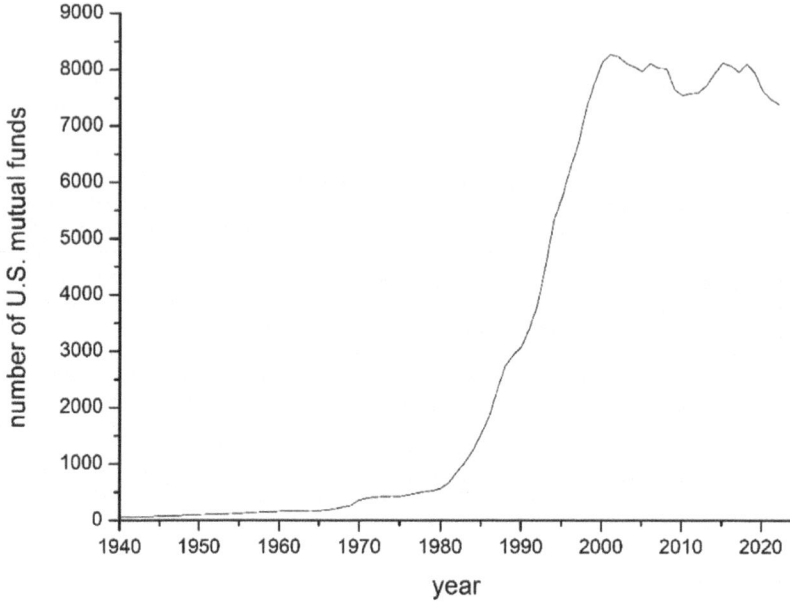

Fig. 1.1 The number of U.S. mutual funds has grown from 68 in 1940 to over 7000 today

question addressed in this book is: how should one select mutual fund/s from among such a large number of possible choices?

It is clear that this question may be important for the economic welfare of the individual investor. It also affects the entire economy: U.S. mutual funds manage $22.2 trillion (see Fig. 1.2), and together with Exchange Traded Funds (ETFs) hold about 33% of the U.S. stock market (see Fig. 1.3). Worldwide, funds manage around $60 trillion (ICI, 2023 Factbook).[1] Investments allocated to mutual funds are conveyed into

---

[1] It is thus not surprising that there is vast literature on mutual funds, discussing the existence of fund manager's investment talent (Sharpe, 1966; Jensen, 1968; Fama, 1965; 1970; Malkiel, 1995; Carhart, 1997; Daniel et al., 1997; Chevalier & Ellison, 1999a; Zheng, 1999; Bollen & Busse, 2001; Kosowski et al., 2006; Cremers & Petajisto, 2009; Fama & French, 2010; Berk & van Binsbergen, 2015; Blake et al., 2017; Harvey & Liu, 2018, 2022), factors influencing the flows in and out of mutual funds (Gruber, 1996, Chevalier & Ellison, 1997; Sirri & Tufano, 1998; Wermers, 2000; Pastor & Stambaugh, 2002; Berk & Green, 2004; Barber et al., 2005; Barber et al., 2016; Kaniel & Parham,

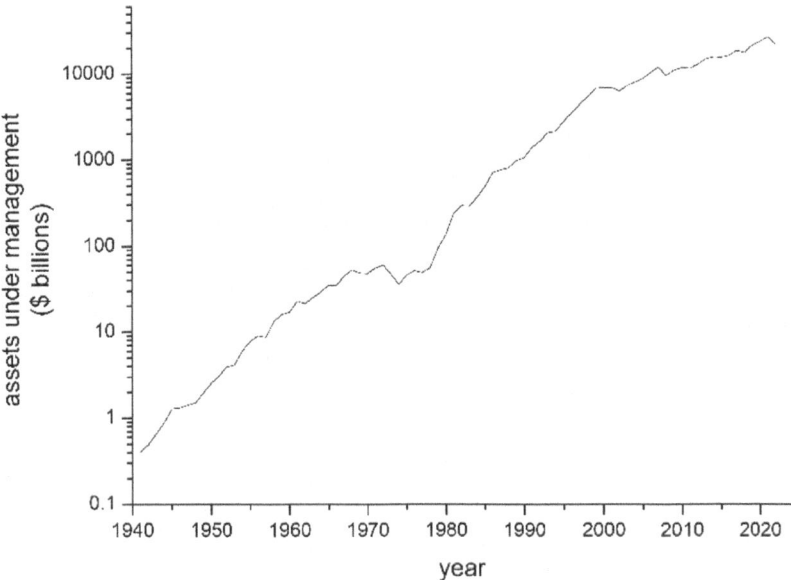

Fig. 1.2 Assets managed by U.S. mutual funds has increased from a few billion dollars in the 1950s to $22.2 trillion as of the end of 2022 (ICI, 2023 yearbook). While we focus on the U.S. market, these trends are global

the capital of firms, and in turn, to the budgeting of projects. Thus, improving the process of mutual fund selection will benefit not only investors, but general economic prosperity.

The foremost problem in mutual fund selection is that future returns are unknown. Investors must estimate (or guess) the future returns and risks of a plethora of funds from past returns (and probably other information). But, past returns are very noisy estimates of the future, as most funds willingly admit.

2017; Ben-David et al., 2022; Mugerman & Steinberg, 2023), the incentives and behavior of fund managers (Brown et al., 1996; Chevalier & Ellison, 1999b; Almazan et al., 2004; Bodnaruk & Simonov, 2016), and the interactions between these and other factors (Berk & Green, 2004, Khorana et al., 2007; Gil-Bazo & Ruiz-Verdú, 2009; Pástor & Stambaugh, 2012; Pástor et al., 2015; Pool et al., 2012; 2015; Berk & Van Binsbergen, 2015; Zhu, 2018; Leippold & Rueegg, 2020; Barras et al., 2022).

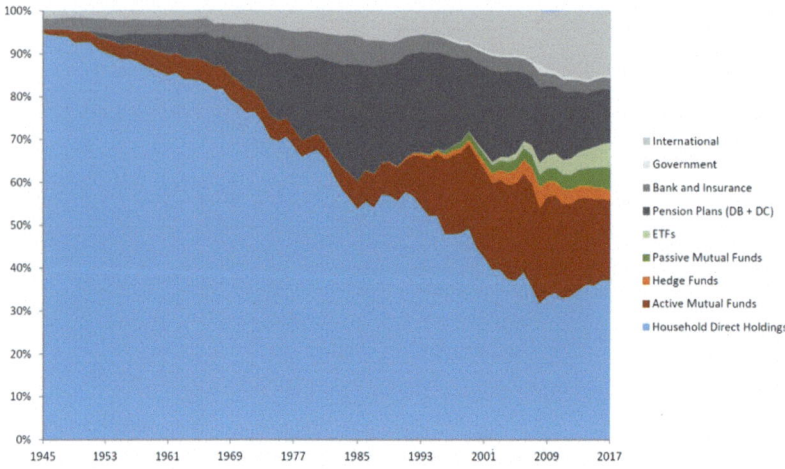

Fig. 1.3 The relative holdings of U.S. equities over time, as reported by Garleanu and Pedersen (2019). In 1980, all funds held less than 5% of the equity market. By 2017, this figure has increased to over 30%

This book provides a method to improve the estimation of the future returns. It breaks down the mutual fund selection problem into two questions:

1. Suppose, unrealistically, that future returns are known. Which performance measure would then be best for ranking funds? Common measures employed include "alpha", the Sharpe ratio, and the geometric mean. Morningstar and Lipper offer additional ranking methods.[2]
2. Since future returns are unknown, what is the best way to rank funds based on the noisy information available?

The first question is about what we should aim to maximize, and the second is about the best way to do this in practice. Chapter 2 discusses the first question in a simple setting where the investment is for one period.

---

[2] All of these ranking procedures will be explained in Chapter 2.

Chapter 3 extends the discussion to the more realistic case of investment for multiple periods. These two chapters show that the *monthly Sharpe ratio* is single most important measure for fund selection. Perhaps surprisingly, this is true regardless of the investor's investment horizon. Chapter 4 addresses the second question: what is the best way to maximize the out-of-sample Sharpe ratio in practice? Chapter 5 discusses the central question of active investing versus passive investing in the market index. Chapter 6 discusses the popular practice of reducing the allocation to equity as one ages, which is the central idea of target date funds, and suggests a simple way to improve this process. Chapter 7 highlights the central and unavoidable role of luck in the investment process.

REFERENCES

Almazan, A., Brown, K. C., Carlson, M., & Chapman, D. A. (2004). Why constrain your mutual fund manager? *Journal of Financial Economics, 73*(2), 289–321.

Barber, B. M., Huang, X., & Odean, T. (2016). Which factors matter to investors? Evidence from mutual fund flows. *The Review of Financial Studies, 29*(10), 2600–2642.

Barber, B. M., Odean, T., & Zheng, L. (2005). Out of sight, out of mind: The effects of expenses on mutual fund flows. *The Journal of Business, 78*(6), 2095–2120.

Barras, L., Gagliardini, P., & Scaillet, O. (2022). Skill, scale, and value creation in the mutual fund industry. *The Journal of Finance, 77*(1), 601–638.

Ben-David, I., Li, J., Rossi, A., & Song, Y. (2022). What do mutual fund investors really care about? *The Review of Financial Studies, 35*(4), 1723–1774.

Berk, J. B., & Green, R. C. (2004). Mutual fund flows and performance in rational markets. *Journal of Political Economy, 112*(6), 1269–1295.

Berk, J. B., & van Binsbergen, J. H. (2015). Measuring skill in the mutual fund industry. *Journal of Financial Economics, 118*(1), 1–20.

Blake, D., Caulfield, T., Ioannidis, C., & Tonks, I. (2017). New evidence on mutual fund performance: A comparison of alternative bootstrap methods. *Journal of Financial and Quantitative Analysis, 2017*, 1–21.

Bodnaruk, A., & Simonov, A. (2016). Loss-averse preferences, performance, and career success of institutional investors. *The Review of Financial Studies, 29*(11), 3140–3176.

Bogan, V. (2008). Stock market participation and the internet. *Journal of Financial and Quantitative Analysis, 43*(1), 191–211.

Bollen, N. P., & Busse, J. A. (2001). On the timing ability of mutual fund managers. *The Journal of Finance, 56*(3), 1075–1094.

Brown, K. C., Harlow, W. V., & Starks, L. T. (1996). Of tournaments and temptations: An analysis of managerial incentives in the mutual fund industry. *The Journal of Finance, 51*(1), 85–110.

Carhart, M. M. (1997). On persistence in mutual fund performance. *The Journal of Finance, 52*(1), 57–82.

Chevalier, J., & Ellison, G. (1997). Risk taking by mutual funds as a response to incentives. *Journal of Political Economy, 105*(6), 1167–1200.

Chevalier, J., & Ellison, G. (1999a). Are some mutual fund managers better than others? Cross-sectional patterns in behavior and performance. *The Journal of Finance, 54*(3), 875–899.

Chevalier, J., & Ellison, G. (1999b). Career concerns of mutual fund managers. *The Quarterly Journal of Economics, 114*(2), 389–432.

Cremers, K. M., & Petajisto, A. (2009). How active is your fund manager? A new measure that predicts performance. *The Review of Financial Studies, 22*(9), 3329–3365.

Daniel, K., Grinblatt, M., Titman, S., & Wermers, R. (1997). Measuring mutual fund performance with characteristic-based benchmarks. *The Journal of Finance, 52*(3), 1035–1058.

Fama, E. F. (1965). The behavior of stock-market prices. *The Journal of Business, 38*(1), 34–105.

Fama, E. F. (1970). Efficient capital markets: A review of theory and empirical work. *The Journal of Finance, 25*(2), 383–417.

Fama, E. F., & French, K. R. (2010). Luck versus skill in the cross-section of mutual fund returns. *The Journal of Finance, 65*(5), 1915–1947.

Garleanu, N., & Pedersen, L. H. (2019). *Active and passive investing*. Available at SSRN 3253537.

Gil-Bazo, J., & Ruiz-Verdú, P. (2009). The relation between price and performance in the mutual fund industry. *The Journal of Finance, 64*(5), 2153–2183.

Gruber, M. J. (1996). Another puzzle: The growth in actively managed mutual funds. *The Journal of Finance, 51*(3), 783–810.

Harvey, C. R., & Liu, Y. (2018). Detecting repeatable performance. *The Review of Financial Studies, 31*(7), 2499–2552.

Investment Company Institute (ICI). (2023). Factbook: https://www.ici.org/system/files/2023-05/2023-factbook.pdf

Jensen, M. C. (1968). The performance of mutual funds in the period 1945–1964. *The Journal of Finance, 23*(2), 389–416.

Kaniel, R., & Parham, R. (2017). WSJ Category Kings—The impact of media attention on consumer and mutual fund investment decisions. *Journal of Financial Economics, 123*(2), 337–356.

Khorana, A., Servaes, H., & Wedge, L. (2007). Portfolio manager ownership and fund performance. *Journal of Financial Economics, 85*(1), 179–204.

Kosowski, R., Timmermann, A., Wermers, R., & White, H. (2006). Can mutual fund "stars" really pick stocks? New evidence from a bootstrap analysis. *The Journal of Finance, 61*(6), 2551–2595.

Leippold, M., & Rueegg, R. (2020). How rational and competitive is the market for mutual funds? *Review of Finance, 24*(3), 579–613.

Malkiel, B. G. (1995). Returns from investing in equity mutual funds 1971 to 1991. *The Journal of Finance, 50*(2), 549–572.

Mugerman, Y., & Steinberg, N. (2023). *How do mutual fund management fee changes impact mutual fund flows?* Available at SSRN 4603217.

Pástor, L., & Stambaugh, R. F. (2002). Mutual fund performance and seemingly unrelated assets. *Journal of Financial Economics, 63*(3), 315–349.

Pástor, L., & Stambaugh, R. F. (2012). On the size of the active management industry. *Journal of Political Economy, 120*(4), 740–781.

Pástor, L., Stambaugh, R. F., & Taylor, L. A. (2015). Scale and skill in active management. *Journal of Financial Economics, 116*(1), 23–45.

Pool, V. K., Stoffman, N., & Yonker, S. E. (2012). No place like home: Familiarity in mutual fund manager portfolio choice. *The Review of Financial Studies, 25*(8), 2563–2599.

Pool, V. K., Stoffman, N., & Yonker, S. E. (2015). The people in your neighborhood: Social interactions and mutual fund portfolios. *The Journal of Finance, 70*(6), 2679–2732.

Sharpe, W. F. (1966). Mutual fund performance. *The Journal of Business, 39*(1), 119–138.

Sirri, E. R., & Tufano, P. (1998). Costly search and mutual fund flows. *The Journal of Finance, 53*(5), 1589–1622.

Wermers, R. (2000). Mutual fund performance: An empirical decomposition into stock-picking talent, style, transactions costs, and expenses. *The Journal of Finance, 55*(4), 1655–1695.

Zheng, L. (1999). Is money smart? A study of mutual fund investors' fund selection ability. *The Journal of Finance, 54*(3), 901–933.

Zhu, M. (2018). Informative fund size, managerial skill, and investor rationality. *Journal of Financial Economics, 130*(1), 114–134.

CHAPTER 2

Criteria for Mutual Fund Selection

Abstract Assuming that the return characteristics of funds are known, i.e. for the time being putting aside the problem of estimation error, what is the best way to rank funds? The main alternative criteria are reviewed. We argue that the Sharpe ratio provides the ranking that is most closely aligned with investors' preferences.

Keywords Sharpe ratio · Jensen's alpha · Treynor index · Geometric mean · Morningstar ratings · Lipper ratings

How should one select a fund, or a few funds, out of the thousands of funds available? Is fund selection a matter of personal taste, or is there an objective criterion for ranking funds? The challenge of fund selection can be broken down into two separate questions:

1. Suppose that future return distributions are known. What is the best criterion for ranking funds? In other words, which of several criteria suggested in the finance literature or by commercial rating services is best aligned with investors' welfare [e.g. expected utility]?
2. In the realistic situation where the future return distributions are unknown, what is the best practical way to rank funds?

Answering the first question, which is the goal of this chapter, will provide a foundation for tackling the more realistic but more challenging second question. The main criteria employed to evaluate fund performance and to create fund rankings are the Sharpe ratio, alpha, and the geometric mean. We begin by describing the theoretical logic of each of these criteria, and then we examine which criteria is most aligned with investors' goals. We will also discuss the popular Morningstar and Lipper fund ranking methods. For further illustrative simplification, this chapter examines investing for a single period. The next chapter extends the results to the considerably more complicated setting of investing for multiple periods.

2.1   The Sharpe Ratio

The Sharpe ratio (initially called the reward to variability ratio) was suggested by William Sharpe in 1966. If (a) returns are normally (Gaussian) distributed, (b) it is possible to lend or borrow at a risk-free interest rate, and (c) investors can hold only a single fund, the Sharpe ratio provides a unique ranking of funds that is perfectly aligned with preferences for *all* investors.

To illustrate this strong property of the Sharpe ratio, consider the two funds shown in Fig. 2.1. Fund A has a higher expected return than fund B, but it is also riskier, because it has a higher standard deviation of returns. Suppose that one has to choose one of these two funds. It may first seem that the choice is a matter of taste: perhaps more risk averse investors would prefer fund B, while less risk averse investors would prefer fund A. But it turns out that *all* investors should prefer fund A because portfolio A^* can be produced by investing some money in fund A and the remaining money in the risk-free asset. A^* has the same standard deviation as fund B, but a higher expected return.

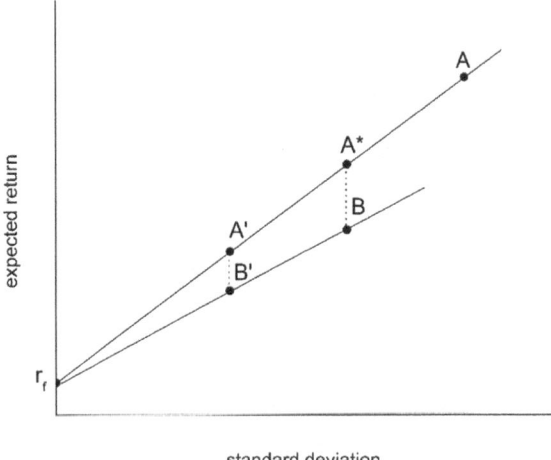

Fig. 2.1 A^*, which is a combination of fund A and the risk-free asset, dominates fund B by FSD. Similarly, for any combination of fund B with the risk-free asset, such as portfolio B', there is a combination of fund A with the risk-free asset, portfolio A', that dominates it for all investors who prefer more over less

For non-Gaussian (Normal) return distributions, one cannot assume that all investors would prefer A^* to B.[1] However, if the return distributions are Gaussian, A^* dominates B by First-degree Stochastic Dominance (FSD), which implies that all investors with a non-decreasing utility function (i.e. all investors who prefer more money over less) prefer A^* over B.[2] This is true not only for all expected utility maximizers, but also

---

[1] If the distributions are not normal, a risk averse investor may prefer an investment with a lower mean and a higher standard deviation than the alternative. Consider, for example, investment A that yields either $6 or $0.01 with equal probabilities, and investment B that yields either $1 with probability 99%, or $100 with probability 1%. A has a higher expected value than B ($3.005 versus $1.99), and a lower standard deviation (approximately $3 versus $9.8). Yet, an investor with a logarithmic utility function prefers investment B:
$EU_A = \frac{1}{2}\log(6) + \frac{1}{2}\log(0.01) = -0.61 < EU_B = 0.99\log(1) + 0.01\log(100) = 0.02$.
This kind of preference ordering is possible only with non-Gaussian returns.

[2] The FSD rule states that all investors with non-decreasing utility functions prefer investment F over investment G if and only if $F(x) \leq G(x)$ for all values of x, where F and G are the two respective cumulative distribution functions [see Hadar and Russell (1969), Hanoch and Levy (1969), and Levy (2016a, 2016b)]. In the special case of

for prospect theory investors who evaluate prospects by the expected value of *change* in wealth (rather than the expected utility of terminal wealth).[3] For any combination of fund B with the risk-free asset, such as portfolio B' in Fig. 2.1, there exists a combination of fund A with the risk-free asset, A', that dominates it. Thus, all investors, regardless of their risk aversion and utility/value function, should prefer fund A.

The point is quite general: if return distributions are normal and a risk-free asset exists, every investor would prefer whichever fund has the highest "slope" of a line that connects the risk-free asset to that fund. The Sharpe ratio is this "slope"; defined algebraically as:

$$S_i \equiv \frac{\bar{r}_i - r_f}{\sigma_i}, \tag{2.1}$$

where $\bar{r}_i$ and σ_i denote fund i's expected return and standard deviation, respectively, and r_f is the risk-free rate of return. See Fig. 2.2, which shows that Fund A is best if no other Fund (such as B) has a higher slope.

This perfect alignment between the Sharpe ratio ranking and investors' optimal choice, for all investors, makes it the unique optimal criterion, at least under the theoretical assumptions of Gaussian return distributions, unlimited borrowing and/or lending, and holdings restricted to a single fund. Section 2.5 below examines the robustness of the Sharpe ratio to relaxing these assumptions.

2.2   ALPHA

Alpha was first suggested by Michael Jensen (1968) as a measure of performance. Jensen's alpha measures the performance of a single asset or a portfolio compared to a broad market index. Although Jensen did not originally frame it this way, the broad index could be an easily investible

---

normal distributions, the criterion for FSD dominance becomes $\sigma_F = \sigma_G$ and $\mu_F > \mu_G$, where μ and σ denote the expected return and standard deviation, respectively (Hanoch and Levy 1969).

[3] The original version of prospect theory (Kahneman and Tversky 1979) allows for violations of FSD, due to the property of subjective probability weighting. As FSD violations are considered unrealistic, cumulative prospect theory (Tversky and Kahneman 1992) corrects this and assures no violations of FSD.

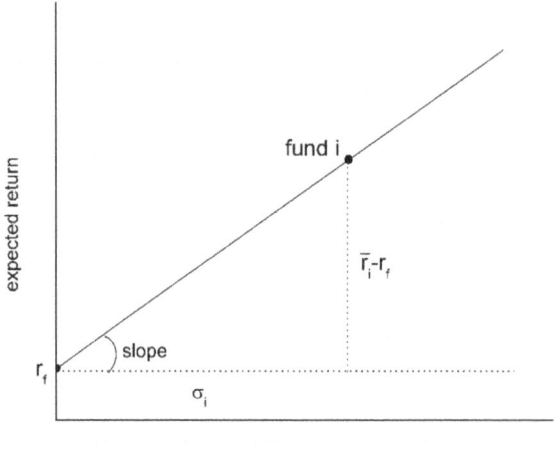

Fig. 2.2 The Sharpe ratio of fund i, $\frac{\bar{r}_i - r_f}{\sigma_i}$, is the slope of the line from the risk-free asset to the fund

passive portfolio such as an "index" fund,[4] which is frequently (though inexactly) labeled as a "market" portfolio. For many investors, an index fund is the passive alternative to an "active" fund, so it indeed plays the role of the broad market.

Jensen's alpha measures the excess average return of an asset relative to the theoretical prediction of the Capital Asset Pricing Model (CAPM) in which the index fund plays its role as the "market". According to the CAPM risk-return relationship,[5] the expected return of asset i should be:

$$\mu_i = r_f + \beta_i (\bar{R}_M - r_f) \tag{2.2}$$

where r_f is the risk-free rate of return, $\bar{R}_M$ is the market (index) portfolio's expected return, and β_i, the beta of stock i, is defined as:

$$\beta_i = \frac{Cov(\tilde{r}_i, \tilde{R}_M)}{\sigma_M^2}. \tag{2.3}$$

---

[4] An index fund is a mutual fund that holds assets roughly commensurate with a broad index such as the S&P 500. It is "passive" because it simply mimics the index and does not attempt any outperformance.

[5] Sharpe (1964), Lintner (1965), Mossin (1966).

Stock i's Jensen's alpha is defined as its excess return relative to the model, i.e. as the difference between the asset's actual average return, $\bar{r}_i$, and the theoretically predicted CAPM expected return:

$$\alpha_i = \bar{r}_i - \left[r_f + \beta_i(\bar{R}_M - r_f)\right]. \tag{2.4}$$

The Jensen alpha can be used similarly to the Sharpe ratio by plotting betas on the horizontal axis and average returns on the vertical axis. The line in Fig. 2.3 connects the risk-free rate (whose beta is zero) with the "market" index (whose beta is 1.0 by construction.) A positive (negative) Jensen alpha implies that asset or portfolio i plots above (below) this line. The slope of a line connecting asset i with the risk-free asset is the popular "Treynor" ratio (1965), an alternative to the Sharpe ratio. The Treynor ratio of asset i is given by:

$$\frac{\bar{r}_i - r_f}{\beta_i}. \tag{2.5}$$

Note that the Treynor ratio is similar in form to the Sharpe ratio, but as it is the slope in a plane where the x-axis is beta, rather than the standard deviation, the denominators of these two measures are different.

Alphas (in the original sense of Jensen, and later extended to various multi-factor models) and the corresponding Treynor ratio have become very popular as criteria for fund selection. They are relatively easy to compute given the selection of a passive portfolio index, which itself serves as a ready alternative for some investors.

However, there are two conceptual problems with alpha as a guide for investors restricted to a single portfolio. First, a portfolio's beta does not necessarily encompass its full volatility and hence its risk of loss. Instead, the volatility is measured by the portfolio's standard deviation.[6] Second, when the market index is an optimal tangency portfolio, the risk-return relationship (2.2) holds exactly, and all alphas are exactly zero (Roll, 1977). Observation of a supposedly non-zero alpha would then be nothing but an estimation error. Parenthetically, such a condition might explain why many active mutual funds struggle to outperform passive

---

[6] If the portfolio is perfectly correlated with the index, beta <u>does</u> measure a portfolio's total volatility (relative to that of the index). This leads to the development of asset pricing theories which explain the expected returns of individual assets that can be perfectly diversified (and hence can be formed into perfectly correlated portfolios).

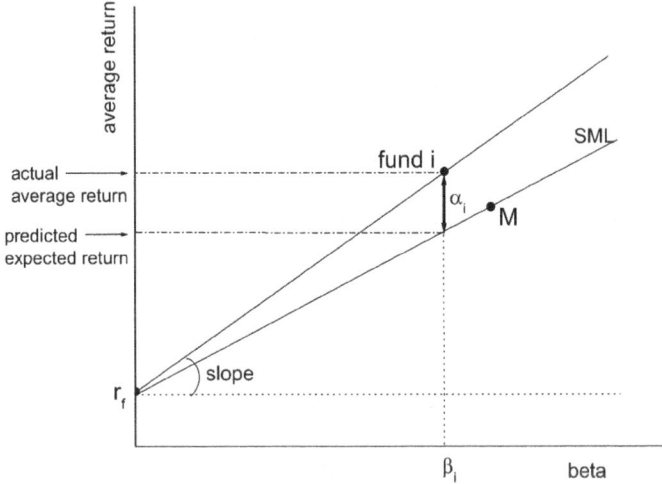

Fig. 2.3 The Jensen α_i of asset i is the difference between the asset's actual average return and the expected return as predicted by the CAPM (Eq. 2.2). Graphically, α_i is the vertical distance between the asset and the theoretically predicted Security Market Line (SML). The Treynor ratio of asset i is the slope of the line connecting asset i with the risk-free asset. Note that the x-axis is different than in Fig. 2.2: it measures beta, rather than the standard deviation

index funds despite apparently superior econometric in-house methods for estimating alphas.

If some assets have truly non-zero alphas, the market index employed is not optimal, and one can obtain a better portfolio (i.e. one with a higher Sharpe ratio), by slightly increasing the portfolio weights of the stocks with positive alphas and slightly decreasing the weights of stocks with negative alphas (relative to their weights in the index portfolio). Formally, deriving the market portfolio's (M's) Sharpe ratio with respect to x_i, the weight, or investment proportion, of stock i in the market portfolio, yields[7]:

$$\frac{\partial\left(\frac{\bar{R}_M - r_f}{\sigma_M}\right)}{\partial x_i} = \frac{(\bar{r}_i - r_f)\sigma_M - (\bar{R}_M - r_f)\frac{1}{\sigma_M}\sum_{j=1}^{N} x_j \sigma_{i,j}}{\sigma_M^2}$$

$$= \frac{1}{\sigma_M}(\bar{r}_i - [r_f + \beta_i(\bar{R}_M - r_f)]) = \frac{1}{\sigma_M}\alpha_i \quad (2.5)$$

Thus, alpha measures the increase or decrease in a portfolio's Sharpe ratio by a marginal change in a constituent's asset investment proportion.[8]

This seems to support common folklore; viz., over-weight assets with positive alphas and under-weight assets with negative alphas.[9] Unfortunately, this advice is valid only for small (technically, infinitesimal) changes in portfolio weights relative to the market index portfolio weights. If an investor holds a single stock, or any portfolio which is different than the market index portfolio, alpha as a positive criterion is misleading.

The following example illustrates this point. Suppose that fund A has an expected return of 7%, a standard deviation of 20%, and a β of 0.5, and that fund B has an expected return of 9%, a standard deviation of 20%, and a β of 0.9. Assume that the market portfolio's expected return

---

[7] Note that both $\bar{R}_M = \sum_{j=1}^{N} x_j \bar{r}_j$ and $\sigma_P = \sqrt{\sum_{j=1}^{N}\sum_{k=1}^{N} x_j x_k \sigma_{j,k}}$ are functions of x_i, ,
(where $\sigma_{j,k}$ denotes the correlation between stocks j and k). We have $\partial \bar{R}_M / \partial x_i = \bar{r}_i - r_f$ and $\partial \sigma_P / \partial x_i = \frac{1}{2\sigma_P} 2\sum_{j=1}^{N} x_j \sigma_{i,j}\sigma_{i,j}$ (the sum of portfolio weights is 1, thus a change in x_i is accompanied by a reverse change in the weight in the risk-free asset; the 2 in the numerator is due to the fact that for each term $x_i x_j \sigma_{i,j}$ in the double summation, there is an equal symmetric term $x_i x_j \sigma_{j,i}$). Equation (2.5) is obtained from the quotient rule $\left(\frac{f}{g}\right)' = \frac{f'g - g'f}{g^2}$. We employ $\beta_i = \frac{Cov(\bar{r}_i, \bar{R}_M)}{\sigma_M^2} = \frac{\sum_{j=1}^{N} x_j \sigma_{i,j}}{\sigma_M^2}$. For an alternative proof showing that a marginal increase in the weight of an asset with a positive alpha increases the portfolio's Sharpe ratio, see Theorem 5 in Dybvig and Ross (1985).

[8] For the tangency portfolio, which has the maximal Sharpe ratio, all the alphas are zero. This is true for any portfolio on the mean/variance efficient frontier, with the appropriate zero-beta rate, see Black (1972) and Roll (1977).

[9] Notice, however, that alpha is a local measure. It points to the direction of maximal increase in the Sharpe ratio for an *infinitesimal* shift in the portfolio weights. Levy and Roll (2016) show that for small but *finite* changes, which are those relevant to investors, the optimal weight adjustments are almost unrelated to the alphas. In fact, in many cases, the optimal adjustment is in the opposite direction of alpha—it may be optimal to *reduce* the weight of an asset with a positive alpha, and vice versa.

is 11%, its standard deviation is 20%, and the risk-free rate is 1%. Fund A has a Jensen's α of 1% $(7 - [1 + 0.5(11 - 1)] = 1)$, while fund B has a Jensen's α of $-$ 1% $(9 - [1 + 0.9(11 - 1)] = -1)$. Thus, ranking funds according to α leads to the conclusion that fund A is better. However, the Sharpe ratio of fund A is only $\frac{7-1}{20} = 0.3$, compared to fund B with a Sharpe ratio of $\frac{9-1}{20} = 0.4$. Thus, as shown in the previous section, all investors with non-decreasing utility functions are better off with fund B, if they must choose B or A.

The CAPM (in 2.2) may be viewed as a 1-factor model, with the market index as the single factor. Since its inception, several additional factors have been suggested as extensions of the model, including the size and book-to-market factors (Fama & French, 1992, 1993), momentum (Carhart, 1997), profitability (Fama & French, 2015), and others.[10] Alpha is extended in a similar way: it is defined as the difference between the actual average return and the expected return predicted by the factor model. A similar criticism applies to these alphas: the alpha of a portfolio, or mutual fund, takes account of the portfolio's exposure to the risk factors (just as the CAPM beta does), but it does not relate to the portfolio's total risk, as measured by its standard deviation. Thus, from the point of view of an investor selecting a single fund, these extended alphas are also not relevant. Section 2.5 confirms this point empirically.

Despite the above, alphas and the Treynor ratio are extremely popular as a measures of fund performance.[11] What is the reason for this? While they may not be adequate guides for an investor selecting a single fund, they relate to the fund manager's skill in producing excess returns relative to the fund's risk factor exposures, i.e. alpha may indicate a fund manager's stock selection and market timing abilities.[12] This has led most

---

[10] Subrahmanyam (2023) suggests that the effect of these factors disappears once they are discovered.

[11] See, for example, the popular financial service Seeking Alpha: https://seekingalpha.com/.

[12] Roll (1978) shows that in this setting, performance may be very sensitive to the benchmark employed.

academic studies of fund performance to employ alpha as the perfor-mance measure.[13] We believe that this academic focus on alpha may have improperly spilled over to the realm of mutual fund selection.

2.3   THE GEOMETRIC MEAN

The geometric mean of a fund that yields a return R_1 $(1 +$ rate of return) with probability p_1, a return R_2 with probability p_2, ... and a return R_n with probability p_n is given by:

$$GM = R_1^{p_1} R_2^{p_2} \dots R_n^{p_n}. \tag{2.6}$$

In the case where all the returns are equally likely $p_i = p_j = \frac{1}{n}$, the geometric mean becomes:

$$GM = \sqrt[n]{R_1 R_2 \dots R_n}. \tag{2.7}$$

The geometric mean has important significance for long-run investors: given a set of alternative funds with i.i.d. returns,[14] the fund with the highest GM yields a higher terminal wealth than any other alternative, with a probability that approaches 1 as the investment horizon increases (Kelly, 1956; Latane, 1959). This strong result has led several researchers to suggest the GM as a criterion for portfolio construction and fund selection (Kelly, 1956, Latane, 1959, Breiman, 1960, Hakansson, 1971, Roll, 1973, Thorp, 1975, Markowitz, 1976, Bernstein, 1976, 2006, Levy, 2015, and Lo et al., 2018). Maximizing the GM also conforms with the objective of investors with logarithmic utility functions, regardless of their investment horizon.[15]

On the other hand, Merton and Samuelson (1974) and Samuelson (1994) object to the geometric-mean criterion and argue that a constant

---

[13] A few examples of this vast literature include Grinblatt and Titman (1989), Ferson and Schadt (1996), Carhart (1997), Baks, Metrick, and Wachter (2001), Cremers and Petajisto (2009), Amihud and Goyenko (2013), Del Guercio and Reuter (2014), Berk and van Binsbergen (2015), Barber, Huang, and Odean (2016), Pástor and Vorsatz (2020), and Sheng, Simutin, and Zhang (2023).

[14] i.i.d stands for identically independently distributed, meaning that the returns on each fund are drawn independently from a distribution that is constant over time. Of course, different funds have different return distributions.

[15] The expected utility of an investor with a logarithmic utility function investing in a fund with equally likely returns $R_1, R_2, \dots R_n$ is $\frac{1}{n} \sum_{i=1}^{n} log(R_i) =$

relative risk aversion (CRRA) investors with relative risk aversion different than 1 (the case of logarithmic utility) will generally choose an investment other than the one with the maximal geometric mean, and this choice holds regardless of the horizon. Levy (2024b) proposes a reconciliation of these opposing views, by showing that a relative risk aversion different than 1 implies paradoxical choices. Thus, while the arguments of Merton and Samuelson (1974) and Samuelson (1994) are undoubtedly correct, they may be economically irrelevant.

The main drawback of the GM criterion is that it does not take in to account the possibility of "mixing" the fund with risk-free asset, i.e. investment in the fund combined with borrowing/lending at the risk-free rate. When such combinations are considered, the fund with the maximal GM does not necessarily yield the portfolio with the maximal GM.

For example, consider the two funds described in Table 2.1. Fund A yields a return of either 65% or -30% with equal probabilities. It has a mean return of 17.5%, a standard deviation of 47.5%, and a GM of 7.47%.[16] Fund B yields a return of either 25% or -6% with equal probabilities. It has a mean return of 9.5%, a standard deviation of 15.5%, and a GM of 8.40%.[17] Thus, if one were to select one of these two funds based on the GM, the choice would be fund B. But suppose that there is a risk-free asset yielding $r_f = 8\%$. Would fund B remain the optimal choice for an investor seeking to maximize the GM? The combination of fund B with the risk-free asset that yields the maximal GM is an investment of 68% in fund B and 32% in the risk-free asset. This combination yields a GM of 8.51%.[18] However, if one invests 47% in fund A and 53% in the risk-free asset, a much higher GM of 10.23% is obtained.[19] Thus, when a risk-free asset exits, the GM criterion may be misleading, even for an investor seeking to maximize the GM. It is interesting to note that in this

---

$log\left((R_1, R_2, \ldots R_n)^{\frac{1}{n}}\right) = \log(GM)$ (where it is assumed, without loss of generality, that the investor's initial wealth is \$1). Thus, fund ranking by the GM is exactly identical to the ranking by the logarithmic expected utility.

[16] $\sqrt{1.65 \cdot 0.70} = 1.0747$.

[17] $\sqrt{1.25 \cdot 0.94} = 1.0840$.

[18] $\sqrt{(1.25(0.68) + 1.08(0.32)) \cdot (0.94(0.68) + 1.08(0.32))} = 1.0851$. It is straightforward to verify, either numerically or analytically, that these are the weights that yield the maximal GM possible for combinations of fund B and the risk-free asset.

[19] $\sqrt{(1.65(0.47) + 1.08(0.53)) \cdot (0.70(0.47) + 1.08(0.53))} = 1.1023$.

Table 2.1   A two-fund example

Fund A		Fund B	
Probability	*Rate of return*	*Probability*	*Rate of return*
½	65%	½	25%
½	− 30%	½	− 6%
Mean	17.5%	Mean	9.5%
Standard deviation	47.5%	Standard deviation	15.5%
Geometric mean	7.47%	Geometric mean	8.40%
Sharpe ratio	0.200	Sharpe ratio	0.097

Fund B has a higher GM than fund A. However, when combined with the risk-free asset, fund A yields a higher GM.

example, fund A has a higher Sharpe ratio than fund B. The following discussion reveals that this is not coincidental.

When a riskless asset exists, the Sharpe ratio is most likely a better criterion for fund selection than the GM, even for investors whose objective is to maximize the GM. Let us elaborate. To a first order, the GM can be approximated by:

$$GM \approx \bar{R} - \frac{\sigma^2}{2},$$
(2.8)

see, for example, Young and Trent (1969), Markowitz (2012). In Sect. 2.1, we show that given a set of funds, combinations of the fund with the maximal Sharpe ratio and the risk-free asset yield the same standard deviation as any other fund, but with a higher expected return (i.e. a point directly above the dominated fund in the mean-standard-deviation plane, see, for example, points B and A* in Fig. 2.1). As the variances of these two portfolios are identical, the combination of the maximal Sharpe fund with the risk-free asset has a higher $\bar{R} - \frac{\sigma^2}{2}$. To the extent that approximation (2.8) holds, this implies a higher GM.

2.4   Morningstar and Lipper Ratings

This section discusses the theoretical foundation, or lack thereof, of these popular fund ratings. Their empirical ability to estimate future performance is discussed in Chapter 4. Both rating systems classify funds into categories, such as "five star", "four star", etc. Each category contains a large number of funds. Thus, if an investor decides to invest in a "five star" fund, there are still dozens or hundreds of funds to choose from.[20]

Morningstar Ratings

Morningstar ratings are the most popular fund ranking system, with a market share of roughly 80%; 73% of the fund ratings advertised are Morningstar ratings (Del Guercio & Tkac, 2008). These rankings were closely aligned with the Sharpe ratio (Sharpe, 1998), at least until 2002, when Morningstar changed its ranking methodology (Del Guercio & Tkac, 2008). Morningstar's current methodology described below is publicly available.[21] The rating is based on the Morningstar Risk-Adjusted Return ($MRAR$), which is defined as:

$$MRAR = \left(\frac{1}{T} \sum_{t=1}^{T} \left(\frac{R_t}{R_f} \right)^{-\gamma} \right)^{-\frac{12}{\gamma}} - 1, \qquad (2.9)$$

where R_t is the return of the fund in month t (1 + rate of return), R_f is the risk-free return, and T is the number of months is the sample. Morningstar only ranks funds with at least $T = 36$ monthly return observations, and when more observations are available, the ranking is based on a weighted average of the score for $T = 36$, $T = 60$, and $T = 120$, depending on the availability of these samples. Funds are divided into the 1–5 star categories according to their $MRAR$ score.

The underlying logic of $MRAR$ is that if $R_f = 1$, $MRAR$ corresponds to the annual certainty equivalent return for a CRRA investor with relative risk aversion $\alpha = \gamma + 1$.[22] Morningstar employs $\gamma = 2$ in its rankings, i.e. the ranking corresponds to relative risk aversion of 3.

---

[20] Of course, this could be the genius of these services; implicitly insinuating that all funds within a category are equivalent, thereby abating an investor's bewilderment over the bedlam.

[21] https://www.morningstar.com/content/dam/marketing/shared/research/method ology/771945_Morningstar_Rating_for_Funds_Methodology.pdf.

[22] The utility function of a CRRA investor with relative risk aversion α is $u(w) = \frac{w^{1-\alpha}}{1-\alpha} = \frac{w^{-\gamma}}{-\gamma}$, where $\gamma = \alpha - 1$. Given a fund with returns $R_1, R_2, \ldots R_T$, the investors expected utility is: $\frac{1}{-\gamma T} \sum_{t=1}^{T} R_t^{-\gamma}$ (where it assumed without loss of generality that the initial wealth is $1). The certainty equivalent return with the same expected utility satisfies

One drawback of the Morningstar rating is that is aimed to capture preferences of investors with a relative risk aversion of 3. Investors with other risk attitudes may rank funds differently. However, this is not the main problem. The main drawback of the Morningstar rating is that, unlike the Sharpe ratio, it does not take into consideration combinations of the fund with the risk-free asset. The following example illustrates this point. Consider fund A that yields a return of either 60% or − 20% with equal probabilities, and fund B that yields a return of either 20% or − 10%, also with equal probabilities. Assume, for simplicity, that the risk-free rate is 0% (i.e. $R_f = 1$). The *MRAR* of fund B is 24.2%, while that of fund A is only 15.3%.[23] However, if one allows combinations of the fund with the risk-free asset, even an investor with a relative risk aversion of 3 will prefer fund A: by investing 50% in fund A and 50% in the risk-free asset, this investor can achieve an annual certainty equivalent return of 72.5%.[24] In contrast, the maximal certainty equivalent return for combinations of fund B with the risk-free asset is 25.9%.[25] Thus, the investor is much better off with fund A, even though it has a lower *MRAR*.

Lipper Ratings

Lipper ranks funds along five different dimensions: total return, persistent return, preservation, expense, and tax efficiency. Each fund is given a grade of 1 (worst) to 5 (best) along each of these dimensions.[26] This multi-dimensional ranking creates ambiguity for the investor. For example, which fund is better, one with a ranking of (3, 2, 5, 4, 1) along

---

$\frac{CE^{-\gamma}}{-\gamma} = \frac{1}{-\gamma T}\sum_{t=1}^{T}R_t^{-\gamma}$, or: $CE = \left(\frac{1}{T}\sum_{t=1}^{T}R_t^{-\gamma}\right)^{-\frac{1}{\gamma}}$. Raising to the power 12 and subtracting 1, as in Eq. (2.9), translates this to an annual certain rate of return.

[23] $\left(\frac{1}{2}\left(1.6^{-2} + 0.8^{-2}\right)\right)^{-\frac{12}{2}} - 1 = 0.153$; $\left(\frac{1}{2}\left(1.2^{-2} + 0.9^{-2}\right)\right)^{-\frac{12}{2}} - 1 = 0.242$.

[24] $\left(\frac{1}{2}\left(1.3^{-2} + 0.9^{-2}\right)\right)^{-\frac{12}{2}} - 1 = 0.725$.

[25] One can verify either analytically or numerically that the combination of fund B with the risk-free asset that yields the highest certainty equivalent is obtained with an investment of 80% in the fund, and 20% in the risk-free asset. In this case, the portfolio returns are either 16% or − 8%, with equal probabilities, and the certainty equivalent is: $\left(\frac{1}{2}\left(1.16^{-2} + 0.92^{-2}\right)\right)^{-\frac{12}{2}} - 1 = 0.259$.

[26] Details on the Lipper ranking methodology can be found at: https://lipperleaders.com/documents/lipperleaders_methodology_us_10mar09.pdf.

the five dimensions or another with a ranking of (4, 4, 3, 2, 4)? The main objective of a fund ranking system is to create an unequivocal ordering of funds, which is obviously difficult in the multi-dimensional setting.

The total return category is simply the fund's average historical return. Persistence is measured by the Hurst-Holder exponent, which is typically associated with return autocorrelations. Preservation is measured as the sum of all negative returns in the sample period. It is somewhat surprising that a direct measure of risk, such as the return standard deviation, is absent in the Lipper ranking. A central disadvantage of the Lipper ranking, which also characterizes the Morningstar ratings, is that it does not take into account possible combinations of the fund with the risk-free asset. For example, one fund may have a more negative sum of negative returns than another, but this may be reversed when combinations with the risk-free asset are considered.[27] Moreover, looking at the sum of negative returns implies that one return of − 10% is equivalent to 10 returns of − 1%; however, risk averters are not indifferent between the two cases, and prefer the latter.

2.5   COMPARISON OF THE DIFFERENT CRITERIA IN A REALISTIC SETTING

Section 2.1 shows that if return distributions are normal, the investor holds a single fund, and unlimited borrowing and lending at the risk-free rate are possible, the Sharpe ratio is perfectly aligned with investors' welfare. Thus, under these conditions, the Sharpe ratio is unequivocally the correct fund performance measure, for all investors who prefer more over less. In practice, none of the above conditions hold. Normality is statistically rejected for the return distributions (Mandelbrot, 1963; Fama, 1965; Levy & Duchin, 2004; Levy, 2024a); borrowing is limited by Regulation T to 100% of the invested wealth; and according to the 2023 ICI factbook, the median number of funds held by investors is 3. The limit on borrowing is not an effective constraint: very few investors lever their investment in stocks, and those who do are typically far from the

---

[27] Consider, for example, fund A with one negative return of − 9%, and fund B with 10 negative returns of − 1%. Thus, fund B has a lower preservation score than fund A. If the risk-free rate is 3%, then investing 75% in fund B and 25% in the risk-free asset eliminates all negative returns. In contrast, to eliminate the negative return of fund A, one should invest at most 25% in the fund (and at least 75% in the risk-free asset).

limit of 100%.[28] The purpose of this section is to examine the robustness of the dominance of the Sharpe ratio over alternative performance measures under realistic return distributions and assuming the investor holds more than one fund.

To examine robustness to the normality assumption, we employ the empirical monthly return distributions. We take all U.S. domestic equity funds in the sample period of April 2001 to March 2021 (240 months). For each fund, we calculate its Sharpe ratio, 5-Factor alpha (Fama & French, 2015), and GM, based on a window of 60 monthly observations.[29] The Morningstar and Lipper ratings are not informative enough to be included in this analysis, as they don't distinguish between all funds in the 5-star rating—their performance will be discussed in Chapter 4. For each fund, we also calculate the maximal expected utility that can be obtained by combining the fund with the risk-free asset. This maximal expected utility is found numerically. We employ the class of preferences that is considered most relevant for economic decision making: Constant Relative Risk Aversion (CRRA) described by a utility function $u(w) = \frac{w^{1-\alpha}}{1-\alpha}$.[30] We analyze the results for a range of values of the relative risk aversion coefficient, α. This expected utility is then translated to a certainty equivalent return (see Footnote 19). Crucially, the return distributions are assumed to be known, i.e. the performance measures and the expected utilities are calculated for the same set of returns. In practice, the challenge is to employ a performance measure based on historical returns to try to predict *future* performance, but this important issue is left to Chapter 4. At this point, we are only trying to determine which is

---

[28] Fortune (2000) reports that the aggregate debt of customers in a large set of broker services is below 10%. For major brokers such as Merrill Lynch, Paine Webber, and Charles Schwab, this figure is below 2.5%. Furthermore, the relatively few investors who do borrow restrict themselves to levels of debt that are typically only 50% of the maximum allowed by Regulation T, i.e. at 50% of their initial capital.

[29] We employ 4 non-overlapping windows of 60 months.

[30] Support for CRRA preferences has been found both empirically (Brunnermeier and Nagel 2008; Chiappori and Paiella 2011; Friend and Blume 1975; Meyer and Meyer 2005; Szpiro 1986a, b; Szpiro and Outreville 1988) and experimentally (Agnew et al., 2008; Andreoni and Sprenger 2012; Heinemann 2008; Levy 1994; Levy and Levy 2021b; Levy and Nir 2012). It is unfortunate that the same notation of alpha is typically used for the relative risk aversion coefficient and to the excess return relative to the factor model. We will be explicit in our meaning where confusion may arise.

the best performance measure, i.e. which is the one that is most closely aligned with preferences.

To obtain statistically robust results, we perform the analysis for a large number of subsets of funds. We randomly draw a subset of 100 funds, and rank them according to either the Sharpe ratio, alpha, or the GM. The investor is assumed to hold the best fund according to the performance measures employed (potentially combined with the risk-free asset), and the maximal possible expected utility is calculated. This process is repeated 1000 times, i.e. 1000 subsets of 100 funds are drawn. The expected utility of each strategy (Sharpe, alpha, GM) is averaged over these 1000 repetitions, and translated into a certainty equivalent return. Figure 2.4 shows the results for a range of different values of the relative risk aversion.

As expected, the certainty equivalents decrease with risk aversion, because the portfolio shifts toward the risk-free asset with increasing risk aversion. The main result is that the Sharpe ratio is much better than both

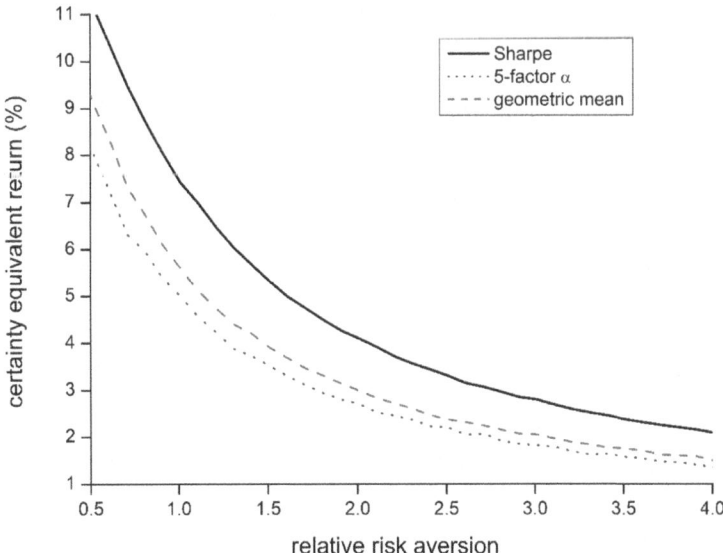

Fig. 2.4 Fund choice by the Sharpe ratio yields higher expected utility (and therefore a higher certainty equivalent return) than both the GM and the 5-factor alpha. This is true for all relative risk aversion values examined. The empirical return distributions, rather than normal return distributions, are employed

the geometric mean and alpha for all levels of risk aversion, even though the return distributions are not normal. This is not surprising, given the results of Levy and Markowitz (1979), and Kroll et al. (1984), who show that the mean–variance framework can serve as an excellent approximation to direct expected utility maximization, even with the empirical non-normal return distributions.

Figure 2.5 repeats the analysis, but instead of assuming that the investor holds the single best fund according to the performance measure employed, we now assume that the investor holds an equal-weighted portfolio of the top 5 funds (again, this portfolio is potentially combined with the risk-free asset). The diversification effect improves the GM and alpha portfolios, but they still substantially underperform the Sharpe portfolio. Thus, the Sharpe ratio is the best performance measure even if the investor holds several funds instead of one, and the empirical return distributions are employed.

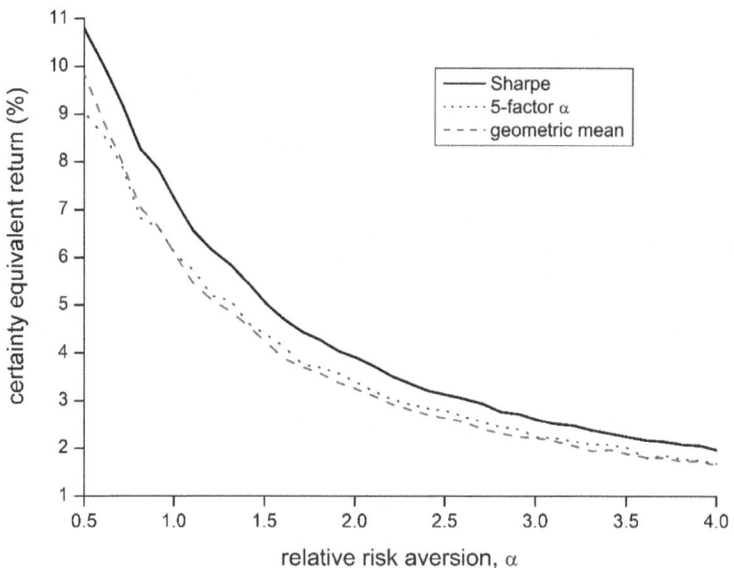

Fig. 2.5 The investor is assumed to hold an equal-weighted portfolio of the top 5 funds according to each performance measure. While holding several funds improves the performance of alpha and the GM, the Sharpe ratio still dominates these measures

2.6 Summary

The goal of a fund performance measure is to create a ranking of funds which is aligned as closely as possible with the welfare of an investor choosing the fund. This is not a simple task, because investors have different attitudes toward risk. The purpose of this chapter is to identify the best fund performance measure under "laboratory conditions" where the return distributions are known, and the investment is for a single period.

If return distributions are normal, a risk-free asset exits, and the investor holds a single fund, the Sharpe ratio constitutes a perfect measure of fund performance. This is true not only for all risk averters, but in fact for all investors with non-decreasing preferences, including those with prospect theory preferences. While none of these conditions exactly holds in reality, we show that the Sharpe ratio is still the best performance measure with the empirical return distributions, limited borrowing, and assuming the investor holds more than one fund.

Alpha is a very popular alternative performance measure. While it may serve as a good measure of the fund manager's ability to produce abnormal returns relative to the fund's risk exposure, which may explain its popularity among academics, alpha is not as relevant to investors who care about a fund's total risk, i.e. the standard deviation of its returns. The main deficiency of the widely used Morningstar rating is that it does not take into account the fact that investors may hold the fund in combination with the risk-free asset. This creates a misalignment between investors' welfare and the fund ranking.

In the next chapter, we consider investment for multiple periods. We show that even in this considerably more complicated setting, the *monthly* Sharpe ratio is the relevant performance measure for long-run investors. The central problem of estimating the future Sharpe ratio from past returns is discussed in Chapter 4.

References

Agnew, J. R., Anderson, L. R., Gerlach, J. R., & Szykman, L. R. (2008). Who chooses annuities? An experimental investigation of the role of gender, framing, and defaults. *American Economic Review, 98*(2), 418–422.

Amihud, Y., & Goyenko, R. (2013). Mutual fund's R^2 as predictor of performance. *The Review of Financial Studies, 26*(3), 667–694.

Andreoni, J., & Sprenger, C. (2012). Estimating time preferences from convex budgets. *American Economic Review, 102*(7), 3333–3356.

Baks, K. P., Metrick, A., & Wachter, J. (2001). Should investors avoid all actively managed mutual funds? A study in Bayesian performance evaluation. *The Journal of Finance, 56*(1), 45–85.

Barber, B. M., Huang, X., & Odean, T. (2016). Which factors matter to investors? Evidence from mutual fund flows. *The Review of Financial Studies, 29*(10), 2600–2642.

Berk, J. B., & van Binsbergen, J. H. (2015). Measuring skill in the mutual fund industry. *Journal of Financial Economics, 118*(1), 1–20.

Bernstein, P. L. (1976). The time of your life. *The Journal of Portfolio Management, 2*(4), 4.

Bernstein, P. L. (2006). The paradox of the efficient market. *Journal of Portfolio Management, 32*(2), 1.

Black, F. (1972). Capital market equilibrium with restricted borrowing. *The Journal of Business, 45*(3), 444–455.

Breiman, L. (1960). Investment policies for expanding businesses optimal in a long-run sense. *Naval Research Logistics Quarterly, 7*(4), 647–651.

Brunnermeier, M. K., & Nagel, S. (2008). Do wealth fluctuations generate time-varying risk aversion? Micro-evidence on individuals' asset allocation. *American Economic Review, 98*(3), 713–736.

Carhart, M. M. (1997). On persistence in mutual fund performance. *The Journal of Finance, 52*(1), 57–82.

Chiappori, P. A., & Paiella, M. (2011). Relative risk aversion is constant: Evidence from panel data. *Journal of the European Economic Association, 9*(6), 1021–1052.

Cremers, K. M., & Petajisto, A. (2009). How active is your fund manager? A new measure that predicts performance. *The Review of Financial Studies, 22*(9), 3329–3365.

Del Guercio, D., & Reuter, J. (2014). Mutual fund performance and the incentive to generate alpha. *The Journal of Finance, 69*(4), 1673–1704.

Del Guercio, D., & Tkac, P. A. (2008). Star power: The effect of monrningstar ratings on mutual fund flow. *Journal of Financial and Quantitative Analysis, 43*(4), 907–936.

Dybvig, P. H., & Ross, S. A. (1985). Differential information and performance measurement using a security market line. *The Journal of Finance, 40*(2), 383–399.

Fama, E. F. (1965). The behavior of stock-market prices. *The Journal of Business, 38*(1), 34–105.

Fama, E. F., & French, K. R. (1992). The cross-section of expected stock returns. *The Journal of Finance, 47*(2), 427–465.

Fama, E. F., & French, K. R. (1993). Common risk factors in the returns on stocks and bonds. *Journal of Financial Economics, 33*(1), 3–56.

Fama, E. F., & French, K. R. (2015). A five-factor asset pricing model. *Journal of Financial Economics, 116*(1), 1–22.

Ferson, W. E., & Schadt, R. W. (1996). Measuring fund strategy and performance in changing economic conditions. *The Journal of Finance, 51*(2), 425–461.

Fortune, P. (2000). Margin requirements, margin loans, and margin rates: Practice and principles. *New England Economic Review, 19*, 1.

Friend, I., & Blume, M. E. (1975). The demand for risky assets. *The American Economic Review, 65*(5), 900–922.

Grinblatt, M., & Titman, S. (1989). Mutual fund performance: An analysis of quarterly portfolio holdings. *Journal of Business, 1989*, 393–416.

Hadar, J., & Russell, W. R. (1969). Rules for ordering uncertain prospects. *The American Economic Review, 59*(1), 25–34.

Hakansson, N. H. (1971). Multi-period mean–variance analysis: Toward a general theory of portfolio choice. *The Journal of Finance, 26*(4), 857–884.

Hanoch, G., & Levy, H. (1969). The efficiency analysis of choices involving risk. *Review of Economic Studies, 36*(3), 335–346.

Heinemann, F. (2008). Measuring risk aversion and the wealth effect. In *Risk aversion in experiments*. Emerald Group Publishing Limited.

Jensen, M. C. (1968). The performance of mutual funds in the period 1945–1964. *The Journal of Finance, 23*(2), 389–416.

Kahneman, D., & Tversky, A. (1979). Prospect theory: An analysis of decision under risk. *Econometrica, 47*(2), 263–292.

Kelly, J. L. (1956). A new interpretation of information rate. *The Bell System Technical Journal, 35*(4), 917–926.

Kroll, Y., Levy, H., & Markowitz, H. M. (1984). Mean–variance versus direct utility maximization. *The Journal of Finance, 39*(1), 47–61.

Latane, H. A. (1959). Criteria for choice among risky ventures. *Journal of Political Economy, 67*(2), 144–155.

Levy, H. (1994). Absolute and relative risk aversion: An experimental study. *Journal of Risk and Uncertainty, 8*, 289–307.

Levy, H. (2015). Aging population, retirement, and risk taking. *Management Science, 62*(5), 1415–1430.

Levy, H. (2016a). *Stochastic dominance: Investment decision making under uncertainty*. Springer.

Levy, H., & Duchin, R. (2004). Asset return distributions and the investment horizon. *Journal of Portfolio Management, 30*(3), 47.

Levy, H., & Levy, M. (2021b). Prospect theory, constant relative risk aversion, and the investment horizon. *PLoS ONE, 16*(4), e0248904.

Levy, H., & Markowitz, H. M. (1979). Approximating expected utility by a function of mean and variance. *The American Economic Review, 69*(3), 308–317.

Levy, M. (2016). *90 cents of every 'pay-for-performance' dollar are paid for luck.* https://corpgov.law.harvard.edu/2016/09/29/90-cents-of-every-pay-for-performance-dollar-are-paid-for-luck/

Levy, M. (2024a). *Mutual fund selection and the investment horizon.* Hebrew University working paper.

Levy, M. (2024b). Relative risk aversion must be close to 1. *Annals of Operations Research, 2024,* 1.

Levy, M., & Nir, A. R. (2012). The utility of health and wealth. *Journal of Health Economics, 31*(2), 379–392.

Levy, M., & Roll, R. (2016). Seeking alpha? It's a bad guideline for portfolio optimization. *The Journal of Portfolio Management, 42*(5), 107–112.

Lintner, J. (1965). Security prices, risk, and maximal gains from diversification. *The Journal of Finance, 20*(4), 587–615.

Lo, A. W., Orr, H. A., & Zhang, R. (2018). The growth of relative wealth and the Kelly criterion. *Journal of Bioeconomics, 20,* 49–67.

Mandelbrot, B. (1963). The variation of certain speculative prices. *The Journal of Business, 36*(4), 394–419.

Markowitz, H. M. (1976). Investment for the long run: New evidence for an old rule. *The Journal of Finance, 31*(5), 1273–1286.

Markowitz, H. M. (2012). Mean–variance approximations to the geometric mean. *Annals of Financial Economics, 7*(01), 1250001.

Merton, R. C., & Samuelson, P. A. (1974). Fallacy of the log-normal approximation to optimal portfolio decision-making over many periods. *Journal of Financial Economics, 1*(1), 67–94.

Meyer, D. J., & Meyer, J. (2005). Relative risk aversion: What do we know? *Journal of Risk and Uncertainty, 31,* 243–262.

Mossin, J. (1966). Equilibrium in a capital asset market. *Econometrica: Journal of the Econometric Society, 1966,* 768–783.

Pástor, L., & Vorsatz, M. B. (2020). Mutual fund performance and flows during the COVID-19 crisis. *The Review of Asset Pricing Studies, 10*(4), 791–833.

Roll, R. (1973). Evidence on the "growth-optimum" model. *The Journal of Finance, 28*(3), 551–566.

Roll, R. (1977). A critique of the asset pricing theory's tests Part I: On past and potential testability of the theory. *Journal of Financial Economics, 4*(2), 129–176.

Roll, R. (1978). Ambiguity when performance is measured by the securities market line. *The Journal of Finance, 33*(4), 1051–1069.

Samuelson, P. A. (1994). The long-term case for equities. *Journal of Portfolio Management, 21*(1), 15.

Sharpe, W. F. (1964). Capital asset prices: A theory of market equilibrium under conditions of risk. *The Journal of Finance, 19*(3), 425–442.

Sharpe, W. F. (1998). Morningstar's risk-adjusted ratings. *Financial Analysts Journal, 54*(4), 21–33.

Sheng, J., Simutin, M., & Zhang, T. (2023). Cheaper is not better: On the 'superior'performance of high-fee mutual funds. *The Review of Asset Pricing Studies, 13*(2), 375–404.

Subrahmanyam, A. (2023). *Keeping it simple: The disappearance of premia for standard non-market factors.* https://ssrn.com/abstract=4584638

Szpiro, G. G. (1986a). Measuring risk aversion: An alternative approach. *The Review of Economics and Statistics, 1986*, 156–159.

Szpiro, G. G. (1986b). Relative risk aversion around the world. *Economics Letters, 20*(1), 19–21.

Szpiro, G. G., & Outreville, J. F. (1988). Relative risk aversion around the world: Further results. *Journal of Banking and Finance, 6*, 127–128.

Thorp, E. O. (1975). Portfolio choice and the Kelly criterion. In *Stochastic optimization models in finance* (pp. 599–619). Academic Press.

Tversky, A., & Kahneman, D. (1992). Advances in prospect theory: Cumulative representation of uncertainty. *Journal of Risk and Uncertainty, 5*, 297–323.

Young, W. E., & Trent, R. H. (1969). Geometric mean approximations of individual security and portfolio performance. *Journal of Financial and Quantitative Analysis, 4*(2), 179–199.

CHAPTER 3

Investment for Intermediate and Long Horizons

Abstract The Sharpe ratio is based on a tradeoff between average return and return volatility, which is fully justifiable when returns are distributed normally. Even if the short-term (e.g. monthly) returns are approximately normal, their distributions become positively skewed as the investment horizon increases, and they eventually deviate substantially from normality. Despite this, we show that the *monthly* Sharpe ratio remains the correct criterion for ranking funds, even for long-run investors. This somewhat surprising result is based on the First-order Stochastic Dominance (FSD) rule.

Keywords Investment horizon · Stochastic dominance · Central limit theorem · Lognormal distribution

The preceding chapter shows that the Sharpe ratio performance measure is best aligned with preferences for single period investments. A "single period" is typically 1 month when measuring fund performance. However, most investments cover longer periods, years or even decades. Is the Sharpe ratio still best in such instances? Should an investor with a horizon of, say, 3 years, rank funds by a Sharpe ratio based on the past series of 3-year returns, calculate their average and standard deviation, and employ the Sharpe formula (2.1) with those 3-year parameters?

There are three problems with this approach: First, it requires a very long historical record. For example, if the horizon is 3 years and prudent estimates should include at least 10 observations, at least 30 years of past returns are necessary. Such data are not available for most funds. Even when they are, 30-year-old data may not be all that related to the fund's present performance. The second problem is that Sharpe ratio ranking can vary with the horizon. For example, fund A might have a higher monthly Sharpe ratio than fund B, while fund B has a higher 3-year Sharpe ratio than A (see Levy, 1972; Levhari & Levy, 1977). This means that there is no unique ranking of funds, but rather there is a different ranking for each horizon. The practical implication is that instead of a single rating of funds, we should have many, one for each horizon. The third problem is potentially the most severe: As the investment horizon increases, return distributions become more positively skewed, and thus deviate more from the normal distribution. Since normality is the foundation of the mean–variance framework in general, and the Sharpe ratio in particular, the theoretical justification of the Sharpe ratio is compromised when the investment horizon is longer.

How, then, should investors with horizons longer than a month select mutual funds? This chapter provides an answer, which may seem surprising at first: they too should rank funds by the *monthly* Sharpe ratio. How could this be possible, given the second and third problems discussed above? It turns out that the problem of increased skewness is actually a blessing in disguise. As the horizon increases, the Central Limit Theorem implies that the return distribution converges to the lognormal distribution (under i.i.d, or even weaker assumptions). With lognormal return distributions, we show below that a fund with the maximum *monthly* Sharpe ratio dominates all others (Levy, 2024). This surprising result has a dramatic practical implication: all investors, regardless of their investment horizon (or risk preferences), should seek the fund with the maximum *monthly* Sharpe ratio!

We begin by discussing the convergence of the return distributions to lognormality. In Sect. 3.2, we review the rules for dominance among prospects with lognormal return distributions. Section 3.3 provides the main theoretical result described above. In Sect. 3.4, we provide empirical evidence confirming the theoretical result, and showing its robustness to introducing serially correlated returns. Section 3.5 summarizes the key message of this chapter. This chapter is more mathematical than the rest of the book. Readers who prefer to avoid the mathematical analysis may chose to skip to the summary in Sect. 3.5.

3.1 Convergence to the Lognormal Distribution

Consider the case of funds with stochastic i.i.d. returns and any 1-period return distributions. The Central Limit Theorem implies that as the horizon increases, the return distributions converge to the lognormal. Let us elaborate.

Denote the 1-period total return (i.e. 1 + rate of return) of a fund in period t by R_t. The total return after T periods is given by:

$$R = R_1 R_2 \cdots R_T = \prod_{i=1}^{T} R_t. \tag{3.1}$$

This implies:

$$\log(R) = \sum_{t=1}^{T} \log(R_t). \tag{3.2}$$

As the R_t s are i.i.d, so are the $\log(R_t)$ s, and therefore, by the Central Limit Theorem, the distribution of $\log(R)$ converges to the normal distribution (see, for example, Fischer, 2011 and references within). If the logarithm of a random variable is distributed normally, the random variable itself is distributed lognormally (see, for example, Aitchison & Brown, 1957). Thus, the distribution of the return R converges to the lognormal. This result can be extended from the case of independent returns to a return processes with weak dependence over time, see, for example, Bradley (2007), Billingsley (2008), and Durrett (2019, Theorem 7.8). Also, the returns need not necessarily be identically distributed (as proven by Lyapunov and discussed in Billingsley (2008)). For example, a fund's volatility may change over time.

The convergence of the return distribution to the lognormal makes the criteria for dominance among funds with lognormal return distributions of central importance for long-run investors. The next section describes these criteria.

3.2   CRITERIA FOR STOCHASTIC DOMINANCE

The mean–variance framework assumes that the return distributions are normal.[1] If return distributions are approximately normal, Levy and Markowitz (1979) and Kroll et al. (1984) show that mean–variance analysis can still serve as an excellent approximation for direct expected utility maximization. This conforms with the numerical results of Sect. 2.5, showing that for monthly returns, the Sharpe ratio is well-aligned with investors' preferences. However, as the investment horizon increases, the return distributions become positively skewed, and deviate significantly from normality (see Table 3.1). Thus, we can no longer employ the mean–variance criterion for dominance, and need to use the more general Stochastic Dominance (SD) framework. Let us first describe the general SD criteria, that make no assumptions about the return distributions, and then turn to their form in the special case of lognormal return distributions.

Table 3.1   Return distribution properties as a function of the horizon

Horizon, T (months)	Mean rate of return (%)	Standard deviation (%)	Skewness	% of funds for which normality is rejected	% of funds for which lognormality is rejected
1	1.13	4.57	− 0.42	87.6	90.3
3	3.47	8.18	− 0.11	98.1	99.3
6	7.22	11.71	0.11	99.1	98.1
12	14.77	18.05	0.34	99.8	97.0
60	106.15	76.79	1.08	100	76.0
120	376.05	470.17	1.93	100	25.7
360	4.94×10^6	7.42×10^7	4.09	100	8.9

The monthly return distribution is taken as the empirical return distribution in the October 2011–September 2021 sample period (120 months). All U.S. domestic equity funds with complete return records are included in the analysis ($N = 5929$ funds). The return parameters reported in the table are averaged across all funds. As the horizon increases, skewness increases, and the return distributions converge to lognormal.

---

[1] Or more generally, distributions of the elliptic family (see Chamberlain, 1983; Berk, 1997). Alternatively, one can assume quadratic preferences. However, these preferences imply increasing absolute risk aversion, which is very unrealistic (Arrow, 1971).

General Stochastic Dominance Criteria

Stochastic Dominance criteria characterize conditions under which all investors of a given class (e.g. all risk averters) prefer one investment over the other. The two central SD criteria, FSD and SSD, are described below.

First-order Stochastic Dominance (FSD):

Let F and G be two investments with any return distributions. F is preferred over G by all investors who prefer more over less (i.e. with non-decreasing utility functions, $u' \geq 0$) if and only if:

$$F(x) \leq G(x) \quad \text{for all } x, \tag{3.3}$$

where $F(x)$ and $G(x)$ denote two respective cumulative distribution functions, and a strict inequality holds for at least one value x_0.

Second-order Stochastic Dominance (SSD):

Let F and G be two investments with any return distributions. F is preferred over G by all risk averters ($u' \geq 0$, $u'' \leq 0$) if and only if:

$$\int_{-\infty}^{x} (G(t) - F(t))\mathrm{d}t \geq 0 \quad \text{for all } x, \tag{3.4}$$

where a strict inequality holds for at least one value x_0. For proof of these results, see Hadar and Russell (1969), Hanoch and Levy (1969), and Rothschild and Stiglitz (1970). The above two criteria are general, and apply to any return distributions. If the return distributions belong to a certain family, these criteria may translate into more specific conditions. For example, if the return distributions are normal, SSD coincides with Markowitz's (1952) mean–variance criterion (Hanoch & Levy, 1969). Section 3.1 shows that the long-run return distributions converge to lognormal. Thus, the the SD criteria under the special case of lognormal distributions are of special interest.

Stochastic Dominance Among Lognormal Distributions

For a random variable R distributed lognormally $\log(R) \sim N(\mu, \sigma)$, the expected value, E, and standard deviation S, are given by:

$$E = e^{\mu + \frac{\sigma^2}{2}} \quad \text{and} \quad S = e^{\mu + \frac{\sigma^2}{2}} \cdot \left[e^{\sigma^2} - 1\right]^{1/2} \tag{3.5}$$

(see, for example, Aitchison & Brown, 1957). Notice that μ and σ denote the expected value and standard deviation of $\log(R)$, while E and S are the corresponding values for R itself. Alternatively, one can express μ and σ in terms of E and S:

$$\mu = \log\left(\frac{E}{\sqrt{1 + \frac{S^2}{E^2}}}\right) \quad \text{and} \quad \sigma^2 = \log\left(1 + \frac{S^2}{E^2}\right). \tag{3.6}$$

First-order Stochastic Dominance (FSD) among lognormal prospects:

Let F and G be two investments with lognormal returns. F is preferred over G by all individuals with non-decreasing utility functions ($u' \geq 0$) if and only if:

$$\mu_F \geq \mu_G, \quad \text{and} \tag{3.7a}$$

$$\sigma_F = \sigma_G \tag{3.7b}$$

(see Levy, 1973, Theorem 4).

Second-order Stochastic Dominance (SSD) among lognormal prospects:

Let F and G be two investments with lognormal returns. Then F is preferred over G by all risk averters $\left(u' \geq 0, u'' \leq 0\right)$ if and only if:

$$\mu_F \geq \mu_G, \tag{3.8a}$$

$$\sigma_F \leq \sigma_G \quad \text{and} \tag{3.8b}$$

$$\mu_F - \mu_G \geq \frac{1}{2}\left(\sigma_G^2 - \sigma_F^2\right) \tag{3.8c}$$

(see Levy, 1973, Theorem 5).

For our analysis, it is helpful to state the above two results in terms of E and S, rather than in terms of μ and σ, as detailed below.

Result 1: The FSD criterion under lognormal distributions can be formulated as:

$$E_F \geq E_G, \quad \text{and} \tag{3.9a}$$

$$\frac{S_F}{E_F} = \frac{S_G}{E_G}.$$

(3.9b)

Proof From Eq. (3.6), $\sigma_F = \sigma_G \Leftrightarrow \frac{S_F}{E_F} = \frac{S_G}{E_G}$. If this condition holds, then $\sqrt{1 + \frac{S_F^2}{E_F^2}} = \sqrt{1 + \frac{S_G^2}{E_G^2}}$, and therefore, again from Eq. (3.6), $\mu_F \geq \mu_G \Leftrightarrow E_F \geq E_G$. Hence, (3.7a) + (3.7b) $\Leftrightarrow$ (3.9a) + (3.9b), and therefore conditions (3.7) and (3.9) are equivalent. □

Result 2: The SSD criterion under lognormal distributions can be formulated as:

$$E_F \geq E_G,$$

(3.10a)

$$\frac{S_F}{E_F} \leq \frac{S_G}{E_G} \quad \text{and}$$

(3.10b)

(see Levy, 1991).

3.3   DOMINANCE OF THE FUND WITH THE MAXIMAL MONTHLY SHARPE RATIO

Empirically observed monthly return distributions are not lognormal: lognormality is rejected for 90.3% of U.S. domestic equity funds (see Table 3.1). However, the Central Limit Theorem implies that the T-period return distributions converge to lognormal as $T \to \infty$. Our goal will therefore be to apply the SD criteria for lognormal distributions to the T-period return distributions. The following result is key to our analysis:

Result 3: Consider two investments, F and G, with any 1-period return distributions, which are not necessarily lognormal, and i.i.d. returns. Then, conditions (3.9) hold for the T-period returns if and only if they also hold for the 1-period returns. Similarly, conditions (3.10) hold for the T-period returns if and only if they also hold for the 1-period returns.

Proof For i.i.d returns, the T-period mean and variance of returns are given by:

$$E_T = E_1^T$$

(3.11)

$$S_T^2 = \left(S_1^2 + E_1^2\right)^T - E_1^{2T} \tag{3.12}$$

where E_1 and S_1 are the 1-period mean and standard deviation, and E_T and S_T are the T-period parameters (see Tobin, 1965; and Levhari & Levy, 1977). Obviously,

$$E_{1F} \geq E_{1G} \Leftrightarrow E_{1F}^T \geq E_{1G}^T \quad \text{i.e.} \quad \Leftrightarrow E_{TF} \geq E_{TG}. \tag{3.13}$$

Thus, condition (3.9a) holds for the 1-period returns if and only if it also holds for the T-period returns. The same is true for condition (3.9b):

$$\frac{S_{1F}}{E_{1F}} = \frac{S_{1G}}{E_{1G}} \Leftrightarrow \left[1 + \left(\frac{S_{1F}}{E_{1F}}\right)^2\right]^T = \left[1 + \left(\frac{S_{1G}}{E_{1G}}\right)^2\right]^T$$

$$\Leftrightarrow \frac{\left(S_{1F}^2 + E_{1F}^2\right)^T}{E_{1F}^{2T}} = \frac{\left(S_{1G}^2 + E_{1G}^2\right)^T}{E_{1G}^{2T}}$$

$$\Leftrightarrow \frac{\left(S_{1F}^2 + E_{1F}^2\right)^T}{E_{1F}^{2T}} - 1 = \frac{\left(S_{1G}^2 + E_{1G}^2\right)^T}{E_{1G}^{2T}} - 1$$

$$\Leftrightarrow \frac{\left(S_{1F}^2 + E_{1F}^2\right)^T - E_{1F}^{2T}}{E_{1F}^{2T}} = \frac{\left(S_{1G}^2 + E_{1G}^2\right)^T - E_{1G}^{2T}}{E_{1G}^{2T}}$$

$$\Leftrightarrow \left(\frac{S_{TF}}{E_{TF}}\right)^2 = \left(\frac{S_{TG}}{E_{TG}}\right)^2 \Leftrightarrow \frac{S_{TF}}{E_{TF}} = \frac{S_{TG}}{E_{TG}}, \tag{3.14}$$

where in the stage before last we make use of relations (3.11) and (3.12). This proves that conditions (3.9) hold for the 1-period returns if and only if they also hold for the T-period returns. The same is true for conditions (3.10), where the derivation of the equivalence of (3.10b) for all horizons is identical to that in Eq. (3.14), with the equality relations replaced everywhere by "$\leq$". $\qquad\square$

Note that SD-lognormal conditions (3.9) and (3.10) imply dominance only if the distributions are lognormal. Thus, in the 1-period, where the distributions are not necessarily lognormal, dominance may not hold even if conditions (3.9) or (3.10) do. Result 3 shows that the conditions hold for the T-period returns (for any T) if and only if they hold for the 1-period returns. As the horizon T increases, the return distributions converge to the lognormal, thus, if conditions (3.9) or (3.10) hold for the 1-period, we can expect dominance (FSD or SSD, respectively) to emerge for T large enough.

Why does this imply that the fund with the maximal 1-period Sharpe ratio is the optimal choice fund for all long-run investors? The last piece of the puzzle is the following result: the fund with the maximal 1-period Sharpe ratio dominates all other funds by conditions (3.9). This is illustrated by Fig. 3.1. In the figure, fund F is the fund with the maximal 1-period Sharpe ratio: $\frac{E_F - R_f}{S_F} > \frac{E_G - R_f}{S_G}$ for any other portfolio G.[2] Graphically, this means that F yields the line originating in R_f with the highest possible slope. For any other portfolio with a lower Sharpe ratio, such as portfolio G, there is a combination of fund F and the risk-free asset, F*, that dominates by conditions (3.9): as F* lies on the line connecting G and the origin, we have $\frac{S_{F*}}{E_{F*}} = \frac{S_G}{E_G}$, and we also have $E_{F*} > E_G$. Thus, F* dominates G by conditions (3.9). This is true not only for fund G itself, but also for any combination of fund G with the riskless asset. Note that the fact that conditions (3.9) hold does not imply dominance by FSD, because the 1-period distributions are not necessarily lognormal. However, as the investment horizon increases, the return distributions converge to the lognormal, while conditions (3.9) continue to hold (as proven by Result 3). Thus, we can expect dominance to emerge. Therefore, with unlimited borrowing and a long investment horizon, we would expect the fund with the highest 1-period (e.g. monthly) Sharpe ratio to dominate all other funds. This holds not only for all risk averters (SSD), but for all investors with non-decreasing utility (or value) functions, including investors with prospect theory preferences (FSD).

When borrowing is limited, portfolio F* may be unattainable, in which case G is not dominated (in the sense of condition 3.9) by any attainable combination of F with the riskless asset. However, condition (3.10) may be met, as it requires less leverage: all portfolios between F** and F* dominate G by (3.10). Again, (3.10) does not imply dominance by SSD for 1-period returns, but as the horizon increases and the return distributions converge to the lognormal, this dominance is expected to emerge.

This theoretical analysis, following Levy (2024), predicts that all long-run investors are best-off by choosing the fund with the maximal 1-period

---

[2] Note that the Sharpe ratio is the same whether described by the rates of return or the total returns, as $\overline{R}_i - R_f = \overline{r}_i - r_f$.

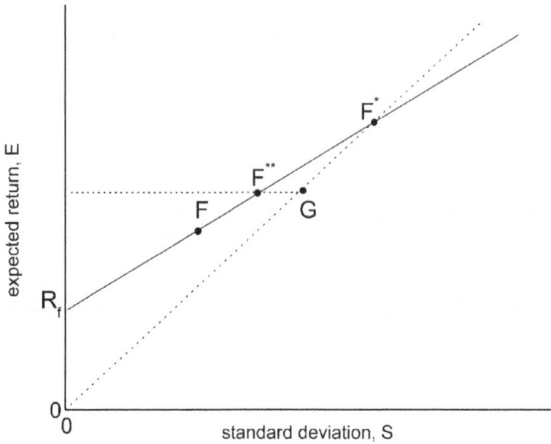

Fig. 3.1 The fund with the maximal 1-period Sharpe ratio, fund F, dominates all other funds by conditions (3.9). For any other fund with a lower Sharpe ratio, such as fund G, there is a combination F* of fund F with the risk-free asset that dominates it by (3.9) (as both G and F* lie on the same line extending from the origin, they have the same E/S). Note that this does not necessarily imply dominance by FSD, because the 1-period return distributions are generally not lognormal. When borrowing is limited, portfolio F* may be unattainable, but portfolio F**, which requires less leverage, may be possible. Portfolio F**, as well as all portfolios between F** and F*, dominates G by conditions (3.10). Note that both E and R_f are in terms of total return (i.e. 1 + rate of return)

Sharpe ratio. In practical applications, the shortest horizon over which fund returns are calculated is typically a month. Thus, in our empirical analysis, we will examine the dominance of the fund with the maximal monthly Sharpe ratio. The theoretical results are based on SD criteria, implying preference by all investors who prefer more over less (FSD), or alternatively, all risk averters (SSD). In the empirical analysis, we will examine the SD efficient sets. Given a set of funds, the FSD efficient set is the subset of these funds, each of which is the optimal choice for some investor who prefers more over less. A fund that is excluded from the FSD efficient set can be safely deleted from the menu of relevant funds, as no investor will choose it.[3] Similarly, the SSD efficient set is the subset of funds, each of which is the optimal choice for some risk averter. The theoretical analysis predicts that both the FSD and SSD efficient sets shrink to the fund with the maximal monthly Sharpe ratio as the investment horizon increases. The efficient sets are constructed by a pairwise comparison of each fund to all others: a fund that is not dominated by any other fund (by FSD or SSD, respectively) is included in the efficient set. The procedure for testing SD when all prospects have equally likely returns is described in Levy (2016), Chapter 5. Note that the SSD efficient set is, by definition, a subset of the FSD efficient set (in the weak sense).

3.4   EMPIRICAL RESULTS

We employ the empirical monthly returns for all U.S. domestic equity funds in the CRSP Mutual Fund Data file in the October 2011–September 2021 sample period. There are $N = 5929$ funds with complete monthly return records in this period. The monthly risk-free rate is taken as the average value over the sample period, which is 0.0447% (corresponding to an annual rate of 0.538%). Recall that we are still in a setting where the return distributions are assumed to be known—the problem of estimation will be the focus of the next chapter. Hence, for an investment horizon of $T = 1$ month, we take the empirical sample monthly return distributions as the "true" distributions.

For longer horizons, the T-month return distributions are generated from the monthly total returns by $R = \prod_{t=1}^{T} R_t$, where the R_ts are total monthly returns (i.e. 1 + rate of return) drawn from the empirical return distributions. In the baseline analysis, we assume that returns are i.i.d., and we create the T-period return distributions by randomly drawing 100,000 vectors of T monthly returns for each fund (with replacement). Thus, we obtain 100,000 T-period returns for each fund, and we employ these return distributions in our efficiency analysis. We later extend the analysis and take into account possible serial correlations by drawing strings of 6 *sequential* monthly returns when generating the T-period return distributions. When comparing two funds, F and G, we consider

---

[3] Fishburn (1974) shows that the SD efficient sets can be further reduced by the convex-SD criterion. We find empirically that the efficient sets shrink to the fund with the maximal monthly Sharpe ratio even without employing convex SD.

not only a direct comparison of these funds, but also comparisons of "mixtures" of the funds with the risk-free asset, including lending and borrowing.

Table 3.1 provides some descriptive statistics about the funds' return parameters at various horizons. First, note that even at the 1-month horizon, normality is rejected (at the usual 5% confidence level) for 87.6% of funds. This does not necessarily mean that mean–variance analysis is inappropriate for monthly returns. As Levy and Markowitz (1979) and Kroll et al. (1984) show, even though the monthly return distributions may be significantly different than normal in the statistical sense, they are close enough to normality such that employing the mean–variance framework serves as an excellent approximation to direct expected utility maximization. This is consistent with our results in Chapter 2. However, as the horizon increases, positive skewness systematically builds up, and deviations from normality become large. For horizons of 120 months or more, normality is rejected for all funds. At the same time, as the horizon increases, the distributions converge to the lognormal, consistent with the prediction of the Central Limit Theorem. For $T = 360$ months, lognormality is rejected for only 8.9% of funds, which is close to the 5% of funds we should expect to reject at the 5% significance level if all return distributions are in fact lognormal.

Figure 3.2 shows all of the funds in the mean-standard deviation plane. Funds are described by their monthly return parameters. Panel A describes the efficient sets for an investment horizon of $T = 1$ month. 85.2% of the funds are included in the FSD efficient set—these are the funds described in the figure by hexagons (blue). The SSD efficient set includes only 1.1% of the funds, described in the figure by stars (red). This result of the SSD efficient set being a small subset of the FSD efficient set is quite typical (see, for example, Levy & Sarnat, 1994). Note that the funds included in the SSD efficient set tend to be those with the highest Sharpe ratios (i.e. highest slopes). This is consistent with the results of Chapter 2, showing that for monthly returns, investors' preferences are aligned with the Sharpe ranking. If return distributions are normal, both the SSD and FSD efficient sets contain only one fund—the one with the highest Sharpe ratio (Hanoch & Levy, 1969; Levy et al., 2012; recall that we are allowing for combinations of each fund with the risk-free asset). We find more funds in the efficient sets due to the fact that the return distributions are not normal, even for monthly returns, as shown in Table 3.1.

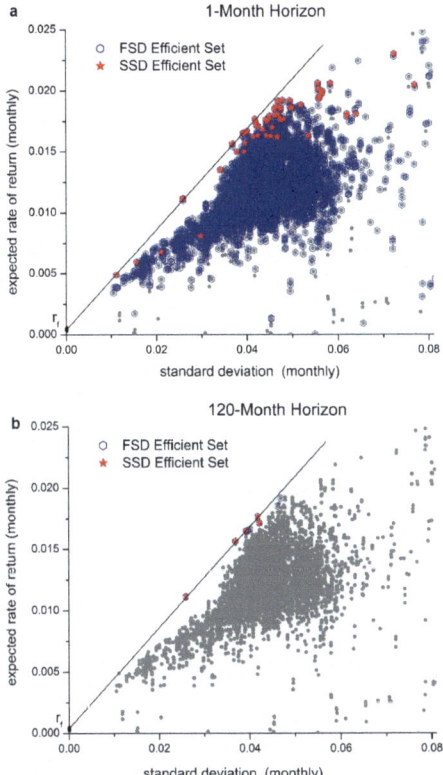

Fig. 3.2 The FSD and SSD efficient sets. Panel A shows the efficient sets for a 1-month investment horizon. The FSD efficient set (funds enclosed in hexagons) contains 5052 of the 5929 funds (85.2%). The SSD efficient set (stars) contains 63 funds (1.1%). Panel B shows the efficient sets for a 120-month investment horizon. The funds are described in the graph by their monthly return parameters (i.e. the location of each fund is the same in the two panels). For the 120-month horizon, the FSD efficient set contains only 11 funds (3 are outside the range of the figure), and the SSD efficient set contains only 5 funds. The efficient funds tend to be those with the highest *monthly* Sharpe ratios

The main question that we ask here is this: how do the efficient sets change as the horizon increases? Panel B of Fig. 3.2 shows the FSD and SSD efficient sets for investors with a horizon of $T = 120$ months. While the analysis is conducted with the 120-month return distributions, generated with random sampling as explained above, in presenting the efficient sets, we still describe funds by their *monthly* return parameters. Thus, each fund is located at exactly the same place in the plane in both Panels A and B of Fig. 3.2. However, as the figure reveals, the efficient sets are different. For the 120-month horizon, the FSD and SSD efficient sets contain only 11 and 5 funds, respectively. Furthermore, the long-horizon efficient sets shrink toward the funds with the highest *monthly* Sharpe ratios, as predicted by the theoretical analysis in the preceding sections.

The shrinking of the efficient sets toward the fund with the maximal monthly Sharpe ratio can be seen more explicitly in Fig. 3.3. The top panel shows the number of funds in the FSD and SSD efficient sets as a function of the horizon. The efficient sets shrink rather quickly: for a 3-year horizon ($T = 36$), the SSD efficient set contains only 9 funds. The FSD efficient set is much larger than the SSD efficient for short horizons of a few years or less, but as the horizon increases, it too shrinks toward the fund with the maximal Sharpe ratio. The bottom panel of Fig. 3.3 shows the average monthly Sharpe ratio of the funds included in the efficient sets as a function of the horizon. The horizontal dashed line represents the maximal monthly Sharpe ratio among all funds, which is 0.414. Figure 3.3 reveals that as the horizon increases, both the FSD and SSD efficient sets converge to the fund with the maximal monthly Sharpe ratio.

The standard mean–variance analysis assumes that the 1-period (monthly) return distributions are normal, and implies that all investors should invest in the fund with maximal monthly Sharpe ratio. The theoretical analysis in Sects. 3.1–3.3 examines the case of long horizons, where the T-period return distributions are approximately lognormal, and reaches the same conclusion: all investors should invest in the fund with maximal *monthly* Sharpe ratio. There are no theoretical predictions for intermediate horizons, where the return distributions are neither normal nor lognormal. However, Fig. 3.3 shows that there is a continuity of the results: the efficient sets converge continuously to the fund with the maximal Sharpe ratio. Thus, it seems that maximizing the *monthly* Sharpe ratio should be the objective of all investors, regardless of their horizons.

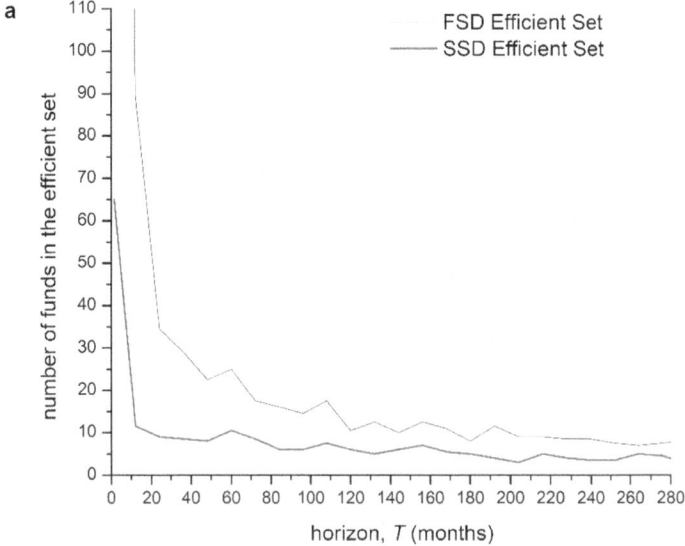

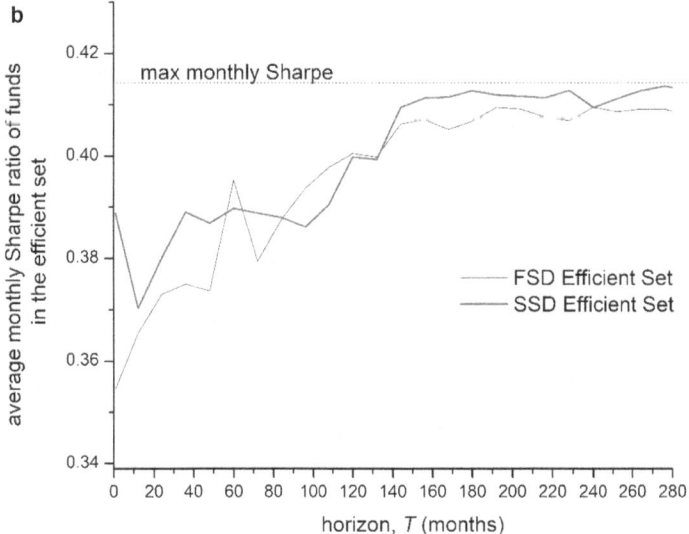

Fig. 3.3 As the investment horizon increases, the efficient sets shrink and converge to the funds with the highest monthly Sharpe ratios. Panel A shows the size of the efficient sets as a function of the investment horizon, T. Panel B shows the average monthly Sharpe ratio of the funds included in the T-month efficient sets. The Sharpe ratio of the fund with the maximal monthly Sharpe ratio is 0.414

To examine whether the results are sensitive to potential serial correlation of the returns, we repeat the analysis, but instead of drawing monthly returns at random to create the T-period return distributions, we draw strings of 6 sequential returns. Thus, this analysis is restricted to horizons of 6 months or more. Figure 3.4 shows the size of the efficient sets (Panel A) and the average monthly Sharpe ratio of the funds included in the efficient sets (Panel B) as a function of the investment horizon when sequential returns are drawn. The results are very similar to those obtained under the assumption of i.i.d. returns: the efficient sets shrink and converge to the funds with the maximal monthly Sharpe ratios.

3.5   SUMMARY

The mean–variance framework and the Sharpe ratio are based on the assumption of normal return distributions. While normality can serve as a good approximation for expected utility maximization when the return distributions are close to normal (Levy & Markowitz, 1979), this is no longer true for the long-horizon return distributions, which are positively skewed and deviate substantially and systematically from normality. Thus, it would seem that Sharpe ratios are only relevant for investors with relatively short horizons.

This chapter shows that, perhaps surprisingly, even investors with long horizons should aim to maximize their portfolio's monthly Sharpe ratio. As the horizon increases, the return distributions converge to lognormality. Employing Stochastic Dominance criteria for lognormal distributions, we prove that as the horizon increases, both the SSD and FSD efficient sets converge to the fund with the maximal 1-period (e.g. monthly) Sharpe ratio. While this theoretical result is derived under i.i.d returns, numerical analysis based on the empirical monthly returns and serial correlations shows that the results are robust to relaxing this assumption. They also hold for intermediate horizons, not only long ones. This implies that all investors, regardless of their utility/value function and regardless of their investment horizon, should choose the fund with the *maximal monthly Sharpe ratio*.

When the return distributions are known, as assumed up to this point, there is no ambiguity as to which is the fund with the maximal monthly Sharpe ratio. In practice, of course, the future return distributions are not known, and need to be estimated. The best way to estimate the future

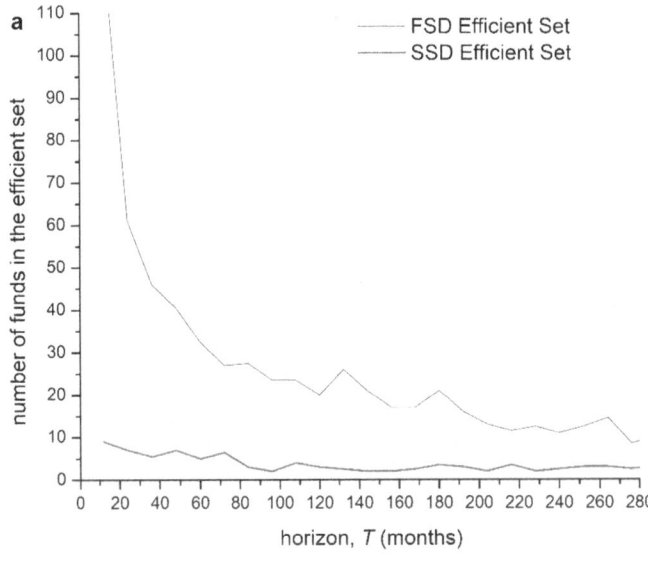

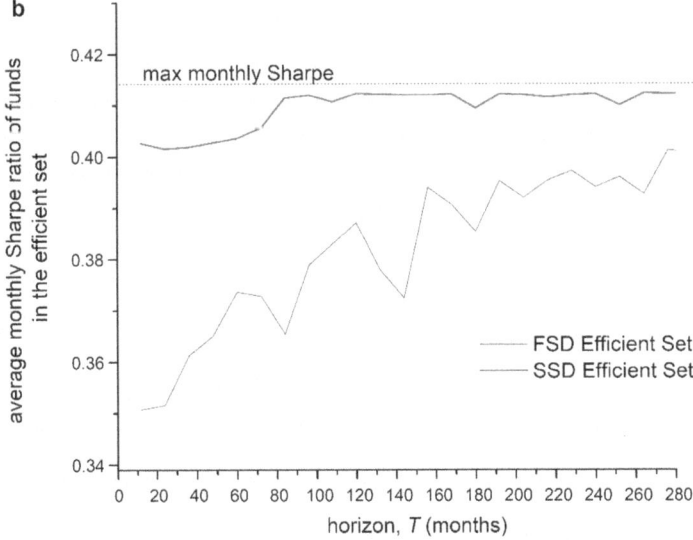

Fig. 3.4 The size of the efficient sets (Panel A) and the average monthly Sharpe ratio of all funds included in the efficient sets (Panel B) as a function of the investment horizon, in the case of correlated returns. The results are very similar to those obtained under the assumption of i.i.d. returns: as the horizon increases, the efficient sets shrink and converge to the funds with the maximal monthly Sharpe ratios. As we are sampling strings of 6 sequential returns, we report results only for $T > 6$

Sharpe ratio is not at all obvious. This is the question we address in the next chapter.

References

Aitchison, J., & Brown, J. A. (1957). *The lognormal distribution with special reference to its uses in economics*. Cambridge University Press.

Arrow, K. J. (1971). *Essays in the theory of risk-bearing*. North-Holland Pub. Co.

Berk, J. B. (1997). Necessary conditions for the CAPM. *Journal of Economic Theory, 73*(1), 245–257.

Billingsley, P. (2008). *Probability and measure*. Wiley.

Bradley, R. C. (2007). *Introduction to strong mixing conditions*. Kendrick Press.

Chamberlain, G. (1983). A Characterization of the distributions that imply mean–variance utility functions. *Journal of Economic Theory, 29*, 185–201.

Durrett, R. (2019). *Probability: Theory and examples 49*. Cambridge University Press.

Fischer, H. (2011). *A history of the central limit theorem: From classical to modern probability theory* (Vol. 4). Springer.

Fishburn, P. C. (1974). Convex stochastic dominance with continuous distribution functions. *Journal of Economic Theory, 7*(2), 143–158.

Hadar, J., & Russell, W. R. (1969). Rules for ordering uncertain prospects. *The American Economic Review, 59*(1), 25–34.

Hanoch, G., & Levy, H. (1969). The efficiency analysis of choices involving risk. *Review of Economic Studies, 36*(3), 335–346.

Kroll, Y., Levy, H., & Markowitz, H. M. (1984). Mean–variance versus direct utility maximization. *The Journal of Finance, 39*(1), 47–61.

Levhari, D., & Levy, H. (1977). The capital asset pricing model and the investment horizon. *The Review of Economics and Statistics, 1977*, 92–104.

Levy, H. (1972). Portfolio performance and the investment horizon. *Management Science, 18*(12), B-645.

Levy, H. (1973). Stochastic dominance among lognormal prospects. *International Economic Review, 1973*, 601–614.

Levy, H. (1991). The mean-coefficient-of-variation rule: The lognormal case. *Management Science, 37*(6), 745–747.

Levy, H., De Giorgi, E. G., & Hens, T. (2012). Two paradigms and Nobel prizes in economics: A contradiction or coexistence? *European Financial Management, 18*(2), 163–182.

Levy, H., & Markowitz, H. M. (1979). Approximating expected utility by a function of mean and variance. *The American Economic Review, 69*(3), 308–317.

Levy, H., & Sarnat, M. (1994). *Capital investment and financial decisions*. Pearson Education.

Levy, M. (2016). *90 cents of every 'pay-for-performance' dollar are paid for luck.* https://corpgov.law.harvard.edu/2016/09/29/90-cents-of-every-pay-for-performance-dollar-are-paid-for-luck/

Levy, M. (2024). *Mutual fund selection and the investment horizon.* Hebrew University working paper.

Markowitz, H. M. (1952). Portfolio selection. *The Journal of Finance, 7*(1), 77–91.

Rothschild, M., & Stiglitz, J. (1970). Increasing risk: I. A definition. *Journal of Economic Theory, 2*(3), 225–243.

Tobin, J. (1965). The theory of portfolio selection. In F. H. Hahn and F. P. R Brechling (eds.) *The Theory of Interest Rates*, MacMillan, London.

CHAPTER 4

Estimating Future Performance: The Shrinkage-Adjusted Sharpe Ratio

Abstract Estimation error is a central problem in mutual fund selection: past return parameters are very noisy estimates of the corresponding out-of-sample parameters. Fortunately, statistical "shrinkage" can improve estimation. The shrinkage-adjusted Sharpe ratio (SAS) is based on the prescription that shrinkage should usually be applied to the gross sample returns, but not to fees, which are typically known. The SAS significantly improves out-of-sample performance relative to existing methods.

Keywords Estimation error · Statistical shrinkage · Fees · Shrinkage-adjusted Sharpe ratio (SAS)

The preceding chapters conclude that all investors, regardless of their risk aversion and their planned investment horizon, should select the fund with the maximal monthly Sharpe ratio. In a happy world where all funds' future average returns and standard deviations are known, this is very easy: just choose the fund when these two parameters yield the largest Sharpe ratio, Eq. (2.1).

Unfortunately, future parameters are not known precisely in the real world. This is a central problem in all of finance, and mutual fund selection is no exception. Future parameters are usually estimated from past returns, but historical estimates are notoriously noisy predictors.

This chapter shows that estimation of future Sharpe ratios can be substantially improved by employing two procedures. The first is statistical shrinkage, which is explained below. The second is the separation of fees, which are typically known in advance, from gross returns, which need to be estimated. These two procedures are combined in the Shrinkage-Adjusted Sharpe Ratio (SAS), which is shown here to predict future performance more accurately than many widely accepted methods.

Section 4.1 introduces the severity of the problem of estimating future return parameters. Section 4.2 explains the intuition of statistical shrinkage. Section 4.3 discusses the idea of separating fees from gross returns in the estimation process. These two techniques are combined to formulate the SAS, which is introduced in Sect. 4.4. Section 4.5 provides empirical evidence about the ability of SAS to predict future performance and compares SAS to other methods. Section 4.6 discusses the robustness of SAS to different sample periods and asset classes. Section 4.7 concludes with a summary.

4.1   Huston, We Have a Problem

A simple method for estimating a fund's future Sharpe ratio is to employ the fund's past (i.e. historical) returns to estimate its mean return and volatility (standard deviation), and then plug these estimates into the Sharpe formula, Eq. (2.1). The problem is that for returns, historical (or in-sample) parameters turn out to be noisy estimates of future (or out-of-sample) parameters. As an empirical illustration, we examine the relation between in-sample and out-of-sample Sharpe ratios for all U.S. active mutual funds using observations from the 120-month period from April 2011 to March 2021 split in half, April 2011 to March 2016 (the illustrative "in-sample" period) and April 2016 to March 2021, (the out-of-sample period.)

Imagine that we are standing in the middle of the sample period, i.e. at the end of March 2016. We observe the historical returns in the period April 2011–March 2016 (this is the in-sample period), but we still can't see the returns during April 2016–March 2021. From our perspective, this second period is "the future", or the out-of-sample period. Our goal is to estimate the "future" Sharpe ratios with the information at our disposal: the returns of the in-sample period. Figure 4.1 plots the actual empirical relation between the in-sample and the out-of-sample Sharpe ratios for these two half decades. Each point in the figure represents one mutual fund. The size of a point depicts the total net assets of a mutual fund as of March 2021.

If the out-of-sample Sharpe ratios would have been exactly identical to the in-sample values, the case of perfect prediction, all points would have fallen on a 45° diagonal line. The picture revealed in Fig. 4.1 is very different: there seems to be only a weak relation between the in-sample and out-sample Sharpe ratios. Funds that have high Sharpe ratios in the first period don't tend to do all that much better than average in the second period. This is true both for large funds and for small funds. The correlation between in- and out-of-sample Sharpe ratios is 0.24. Even this unimpressive relation is partly attributable to funds performing worst in-sample; such funds tend to continue to perform poorly out-of-sample: if funds with negative in-sample Sharpe ratios are excluded, the correlation is reduced to 0.17. This resonates with Lo's (2002) analysis, showing

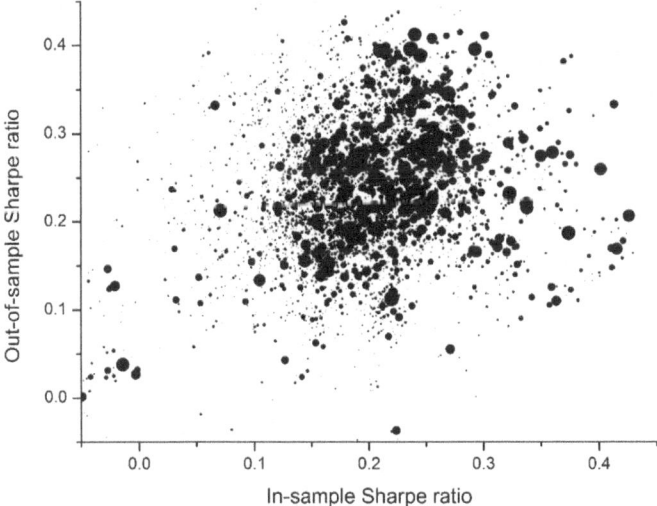

Fig. 4.1 Out-of-sample versus in-sample ratios Sharpe ratios. All active funds with complete return records over the April 2011–March 2021 120-month period are shown. In-sample (i.e. "past") Sharpe ratios are calculated employing the first 60 months, and out-of-sample (i.e. "future") ratios are based on the subsequent 60 months. Circle sizes are proportional to fund size (total net assets as of March 2021)

that the errors in estimating Sharpe ratios can be in the same order of magnitude as the ratios themselves.

Because the picture at the individual fund level is very noisy, as evident from Fig. 4.1, researchers often group funds into deciles in an attempt to detect patterns that are not perceptible at the individual fund level. Figure 4.2 depicts the results of such an approach. Funds are sorted into deciles by their in-sample Sharpe ratios. For each decile, the (equal-weighted) average in-sample and out-of-sample Sharpe ratios are calculated for all funds included in the decile. While this clears up the picture relative to Fig. 4.1, it still reveals that there is almost no relation between the in-sample and out-of-sample Sharpe ratios, except for the worst performing funds, that tend to persist in poor performance.

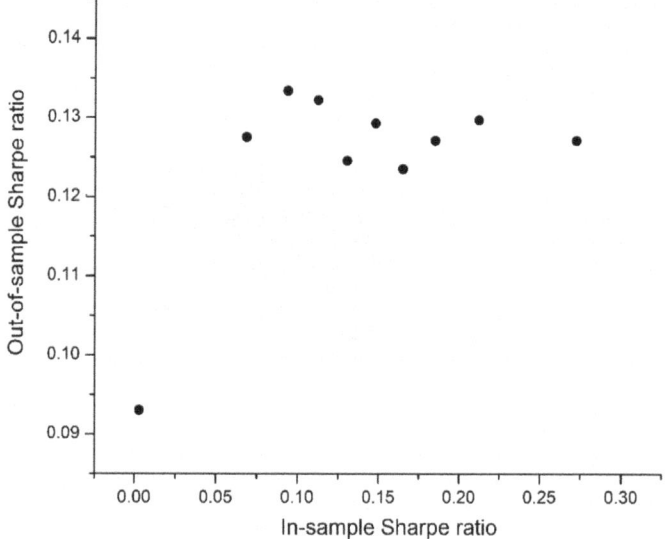

Fig. 4.2 Funds are sorted into deciles by their in-sample Sharpe ratio. The equal-weighted average out-of-sample Sharpe ratio is shown as a function of the average in-sample ratio. There is almost no relation between the in-sample and out-of-sample Sharpe ratios, except for the worst performing funds in-sample, that tend to persist in their poor performance in the out-of-sample period

The picture that emerges from Figs. 4.1 and 4.2 is quite bleak: it seems that the Sharpe ratios based on past returns provide almost zero predictive power about the future performance. Unfortunately, this pessimistic result is also true for alternative performance measures such as alphas and Morningstar ratings. In an influential paper, Carhart (1997) measures fund performance by alpha and finds very weak relation between the in-sample performance and the out-of-sample performance. His conclusions are consistent with the picture in Fig. 4.2:

> "The only significant persistence not explained is concentrated in strong underperformance by the worst-return mutual funds. The results do not support the existence of skilled or informed mutual fund portfolio managers." (Carhart, 1997, p. 57).

Gruber (1996), Zheng (1999), and Bollen and Busse (2001) reach similar conclusions. Philips and Kinniry (2010) examine the ability of Morningstar ratings to predict future performance. They find that:

> "...a given rating offers little information about expected future relative performance; in fact, our analysis reveals that higher-rated funds are no more likely to outperform a given benchmark than lower-rated funds..." (p. 1).

They conclude:

> "...quantitatively based rating systems do a tremendous job of explaining past performance, but generally offer little insight into future performance." (p. 9).

This is a very troubling picture: millions of households invest trillions of dollars based on past performance, which is not very indicative of future performance. Fortunately, one can do better than base prediction on the in-sample Sharpe ratio by employing shrinkage, as described below.

4.2   THE IDEA OF SHRINKAGE

Suppose that we are attempting to estimate the IQ of a person that we are considering to hire. We can't directly observe this number, but we do have a noisy measure of it: the score the person achieved in an IQ test. This measure is noisy, because it is possible, for example, that the person guessed the answers in a few multiple-choice questions and got lucky, in which case his test score is higher than his actual IQ. An opposite error is also possible: it is possible that the person had a "bad day", and his test score is lower than his actual IQ. For simplicity, let's assume that these two errors are symmetric and a-priori equally likely. For concreteness, assume that unconditionally, there is a 50% chance for the case where the test score is 10 points higher than the actual IQ, and a 50% chance that it is 10 points lower than the actual IQ. Suppose that the individual we are considering has a test score of 130. What should be our best estimate of his actual IQ?

As the two kinds of error are unconditionally equally likely, the natural answer to this question is 130. However, closer consideration reveals that this is not necessarily true. There are two possible cases: the first is that the actual IQ is 120 and the person "got lucky"; the second is that the actual IQ is 140 and the person had a "bad day". While the two errors are unconditionally equally likely, given the test score of 130, the first case is more likely, simply because there are more people in the population with IQ 120 than there are with IQ 140. Thus, we should adjust our estimate to be lower than 130. Figure 4.3 illustrates this point. Similarly, if another person has a test score of 70, we should adjust our estimate to be higher than 70, because there are more people with IQ 80 than there are with IQ 60. The result is that we "shrink" our estimates toward the cross-section average (in the case of IQ scores, toward 100).

This is the basic intuition for the statistical theory of shrinkage, developed by James and Stein (1961). The exact formulas for shrinkage depend on the distribution of the quantity (e.g. IQ) in the population, and the nature of the noise. Shrinkage should be applied to the estimation of any variable that we measure with estimation error. In the realm of finance, shrinkage is usually employed in the estimation of expected returns for portfolio optimization (Jorion, 1986), and in the estimation of betas (Levi & Welch, 2017; Vasicek, 1973).[1]

---

[1] Bloomberg employs the following shrinkage formula for betas: $\beta_i = \frac{2}{3} \cdot b_i + \frac{1}{3} \cdot 1$, where b_i is the sample beta and β_i is Bloomberg's estimate of the true value. Thus, all sample betas are shrunk by a factor of $\frac{1}{3}$ toward the cross-sectional (value-weighted) average beta of 1. This is an over-simplification, because it applies the same shrinkage intensity to all stocks. Vasicek (1973) shows that more shrinkage should be applied to stocks with higher residual variances.

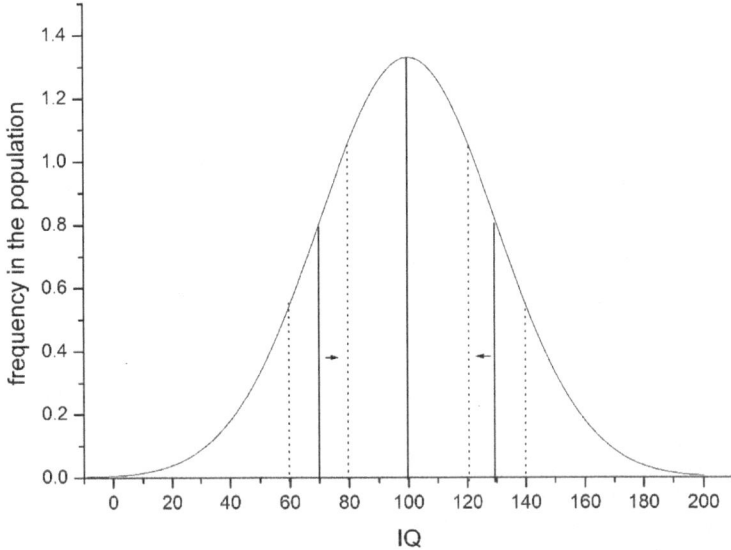

Fig. 4.3 The idea of shrinkage. An IQ test score of 130 can be the result of a true IQ of 120 and "good luck", or a true IQ of 140 and a "bad day". Even if the errors are unconditionally symmetric, the first case is more likely, simply because there are more people with an IQ of 120 than there are with an IQ of 140, as shown by the dotted lines. Thus, our best estimate of the IQ of a person with a test score of 130 should be somewhat lower than 130. Similarly, our best estimate of the IQ of a person with a test score of 70 should be somewhat *higher* than 70. Thus, we "shrink" our estimates toward the cross-sectional average IQ of 100

The noisier the estimation, the less we can trust the sample information, and the more shrinkage we apply. The error in estimating a fund's mean return is related to its volatility—the higher the volatility, the larger the estimation error, and the higher the intensity of shrinkage that should be applied. This implies that shrinkage does not necessarily preserve the ranking of funds. For example, suppose that fund A has a sample average return of 16% and a sample standard deviation of 30%, while fund B has a sample average return of 15% and a sample standard deviation of 20%. Assume that the average return across all funds, i.e. the shrinkage target, is 12%. It is certainly possible that our shrinkage-adjusted estimate of the mean return of fund A will be lower than that of fund B, because of A's larger volatility.

4.3   FEES SHOULD BE TREATED SEPARATELY

Investors are naturally interested in fund returns net of fees. Therefore, most performance measures are based on the sample net returns, i.e. the gross returns minus fees. This implicitly assigns the same weight to the gross returns and to fees. We argue that fees should be separated from the gross returns, and treated separately. To illustrate why, consider the following example. Fund A has a sample average annual gross return of 11% and charges annual fees of 1%. Fund B has a sample average gross return of 12% and charges fees of 2%. Assume for simplicity that the two funds have the same volatility. Which fund should the investor prefer? At first glance, it may seem that the two funds are equivalent, because they both yield an average net return of 10%. Note, however, that the sample average gross returns are noisy, while the fees are known.[2] Intuitively, this suggests that fees should be weighted more heavily than sample returns. In the extreme case in which the sample gross returns are completely uninformative, one should ignore them altogether and rank funds only according to fees. In the more realistic and interesting case, where the sample gross return is a noisy signal about future returns, sample gross returns should be considered, but they should be under-weighted relative to the known fees.

The Shrinkage-Adjusted Sharpe Ratio (SAS) derived below captures this idea. It applies shrinkage to the sample gross returns, and only then subtracts fees. Thus, the sample gross returns are shrunk, while fees are not. This is in contrast to the standard practice of either not using shrinkage at all, or applying shrinkage to the sample net returns, i.e. applying the same shrinkage to gross returns and to fees.

---

[2] Fees may also change, but they are typically very stable over time. For example, the standard deviation in monthly fees is lower than 0.01% for 88% of U.S. domestic equity funds. It is lower than 0.02% for 97% of funds (for the 2012–2021 sample period). These standard deviations are approximately one tenth and one fifth of the average level of monthly fees, which is about 0.1%. This variation in fees is very low compared to the variation of monthly returns, with a typical average return of 1% and a standard deviation of about 4%.

4.4 THE SHRINKAGE-ADJUSTED SHARPE RATIO (SAS)

Consider an investor who observes T returns of fund i, with a sample gross mean $\overline{R}_i$. All returns are in excess of the risk-free rate. According to Bayes' theorem, the investor forms her posterior belief regarding the expected gross return based on the sample mean and the investor's prior belief. The prior could be, for example, the cross-sectional mean return. For normally distributed returns, and a normal prior with mean μ and standard deviation σ_μ, the investor's posterior expected gross return for fund i is given by:

$$E\left(\mu_i | \overline{R}_i^{\text{gross}}\right) = \frac{\frac{T}{\sigma_i^2}\overline{R}_i^{\text{gross}} + \frac{1}{\sigma_\mu^2}\mu}{\left(\frac{T}{\sigma_i^2} + \frac{1}{\sigma_\mu^2}\right)}, \qquad (4.1)$$

where σ_i is the standard deviation of fund i's returns (see, for example, Lee, 2012, p. 46). Equation (4.1) can be written as:

$$E\left(\mu_i | \overline{R}_i^{\text{gross}}\right) = \gamma_i \overline{R}_i^{\text{gross}} + (1 - \gamma_i)\mu, \qquad (4.2)$$

where γ_i, which can be viewed as a fund-specific shrinkage factor, is given by:

$$\gamma_i \equiv \frac{\frac{T}{\sigma_i^2}}{\frac{T}{\sigma_i^2} + \frac{1}{\sigma_\mu^2}} = \frac{1}{1 + \frac{\sigma_i^2}{T\sigma_\mu^2}}. \qquad (4.3)$$

γ_i determines how much the sample average return is shrunk toward the prior. Equation (4.2) manifests the idea of shrinkage: the ex-ante gross return of fund i is estimated as a weighted average of the fund's sample gross return, and the cross-sectional average return of all funds. The higher the standard deviation of fund i, the more noisy its sample estimate, and therefore, the less weight is attached to its sample return [i.e. a high σ_i implies a low γ_i, see Eq. (4.3)]. $\gamma_i = 1$ implies no shrinkage at all, while on the other extreme $\gamma_i = 0$ implies that the sample returns are completely ignored. Equation (4.1) is quite standard, see, for example, Lee (2012) and references therein.

The non-standard suggestion here (following Levy & Roll, 2018, 2023) is separating gross returns from fees, and applying shrinkage only to the gross returns. The derivation of Eq. (4.1) assumes that the return distributions are normal, and, perhaps more importantly, that fund returns are drawn from a distribution that is stable over time. This is the setup employed by Levy and Roll (2018). In practice, these assumptions do not hold, and a better estimation of the fund's future expected return may be obtained with a higher (or lower) shrinkage intensity (i.e. with a lower or higher value of γ_i). This is an issue investigated empirically in Sect. 4.5. In order to allow for "extra shrinkage" relative to Eqs. (4.2–4.3), we introduce a market-wide shrinkage parameter γ_μ defined on the interval [0, 1], and we generalize Eq. (4.3) to:

$$\gamma_i = \frac{1}{1 + \frac{\sigma_i^2}{T\sigma_\mu^2}\left(\frac{1}{\gamma_\mu} - 1\right)} \qquad (4.4)$$

For $\gamma_\mu = \frac{1}{2}$, the standard Eq. (4.3) is obtained as a special case. Values of γ_μ lower than $\frac{1}{2}$ imply more shrinkage relative to Eq. (4.3) (i.e. a lower γ_i), and values higher than $\frac{1}{2}$ imply less shrinkage. In the extremes, $\gamma_\mu = 0$ implies $\gamma_i = 0$, i.e. this is the case of maximal shrinkage where the sample average return is completely ignored; $\gamma_\mu = 1$ implies $\gamma_i = 1$, i.e. the case of no shrinkage at all. In our empirical analysis, we will investigate the value of γ_μ that yields the best out-of-sample performance prediction.[3]

Our goal is an estimate of the fund's Sharpe ratio, i.e. the expected net return (net of fees and in excess of the risk-free rate), divided by the standard deviation of returns. In their analysis, Levy and Roll (2018) assume that the standard deviation is known. In practice, of course, the standard deviation is also measured with error, and shrinkage in the sense of James and Stein (1961) may provide a better estimate of the out-of-sample standard deviation than the sample standard deviation. We employ the following estimate of the fund's standard deviation:

$$\sigma_i = \gamma_\sigma \hat{\sigma}_i + (1 - \gamma_\sigma)\overline{\sigma}, \qquad (4.5)$$

where $\hat{\sigma}_i$ is the sample standard deviation of fund i, $\overline{\sigma}$ is the average standard deviation across all funds, and γ_σ determines the shrinkage intensity for the standard deviations. Following Levy and Roll (2023), the

---

[3] Levi and Welch (2017) employ a similar approach in estimating betas.

Shrinkage Adjusted Sharpe Ratio (SAS) of fund i is thus given by:

$$SAS_i = \frac{\gamma_i \overline{R_i^{\text{gross}}} + (1 - \gamma_i)\mu - fee_i}{\gamma_\sigma \hat{\sigma}_i + (1 - \gamma_\sigma)\overline{\sigma}} \tag{4.6}$$

where $\overline{R_i^{\text{gross}}}$ is the fund's average sample gross return (in excess of the risk-free rate), and γ_i is given by Eq. (4.4), i.e. it is determined by the parameter γ_μ. Thus, the SAS formula depends on the two market-wide (rather than fund-specific) shrinkage intensities, γ_μ and γ_σ. The standard sample Sharpe ratio is obtained as a special case with $\gamma_\mu = 1$ and $\gamma_\sigma = 1$. The analysis of Levy and Roll (2018) can be viewed as a special case with $\gamma_\mu = \frac{1}{2}$ and $\gamma_\sigma = 1$. As the return distributions may change over time, by a process that is unknown, and as the distributions are not necessarily normal, the optimal values of γ_μ and γ_σ cannot be derived analytically. In the next section, we empirically examine which combination of γ_μ and γ_σ provides the best fund ranking, in the sense of providing the best prediction of future performance.

4.5   EMPIRICAL ANALYSIS

Our main analysis is conducted on all U.S. domestic equity funds. As a robustness test, in the next section, we also separately examine all foreign equity funds, plus corporate and municipal fixed-income funds. We employ data from the CRSP survivorship-bias-free Mutual Fund Database. Monthly fee data are mostly unavailable before December 1991, and we take the sample period of December 1991–September 2021 (358 months). Monthly risk-free rates are taken from the CRSP Monthly Risk-free Series.

We evaluate performance measures by employing two approaches. In the first approach, we examine the out-of-sample performance of the *top funds* that are ranked highest by the in-sample measure. These are arguably a prime focus of investors. In the second approach, we evaluate performance by looking at the relationship between the in-sample ranking and out-of-sample performance for *all funds*, similar to the decile analysis in Fig. 4.2. This provides a wider perspective on the ranking of funds, and has the statistical advantage of employing data for all funds, not just the top funds.

At month t, the in-sample SAS (Eq. 4.6) is computed over the preceding T months, $t - T$ to $t - 1$, for each available fund; we employ

$T = 60$ months in our main analysis. (The robustness test reported in the next section uses $T = 36$ as an alternative). $\overline{R}_i^{\text{gross}}$ and $\hat{\sigma}_i$ are the sample average return in excess of the risk-free rate, gross of fees, and the sample standard deviation of fund i, respectively. σ_μ, the cross-sectional standard deviation of mean returns across all funds (Eqs. 4.3–4.4), is estimated by its sample value. Similarly, $\overline{\sigma}$ (Eq. 4.5) is taken as the average of sample standard deviations across all funds while μ, the mean prior expected return (Eq. 4.1), is taken as the average return of the market portfolio in excess of the risk-free rate over the entire 1991–2021 sample period, which is 0.77%.

The SAS depends on the intensity of shrinkage employed, i.e. on the parameters γ_μ and γ_σ. As admitted above, the optimal values of these parameters depend on the unknown stability of the return generating process. Our goal is to find the combination of γ_μ and γ_σ that provides the most informative fund ranking, i.e. the combination that delivers the best out-of-sample performance.

For our top fund approach, each combination of γ_μ and γ_σ selects the ten funds with the highest in-sample SAS. This is then linked to an out-of-sample Sharpe ratio (net of fees) from holding these same ten funds equally weighted over the next year. At the end of the year, the process is repeated: we again calculate the SAS for all funds, and choose the top 10 funds according to the updated in-sample SAS values. This is repeated over the entire 1991–2021 sample period. Figure 4.4 shows the out-of-sample monthly Sharpe ratio (of net returns), calculated over the entire sample period, for each $(\gamma_\mu, \gamma_\sigma)$ combination (γ_μ and γ_σ are varied from 0 to 1 at increments of 0.01, thus a total of $101^2 = 10,201$ combinations are evaluated). The colors (shades) in the map indicate the out-of-sample Sharpe ratio for each $(\gamma_\mu, \gamma_\sigma)$ combination. Brighter colors (lighter shades) correspond to better performance, as indicated by the legend (vertical color bar) to the right of the figure.

Note that the case $(\gamma_\mu = 1, \gamma_\sigma = 1)$, which is shown by the top right corner of the figure, implies no shrinkage at all. This corresponds to the widespread practice of employing the sample Sharpe ratios. This strategy yields an out-of-sample Sharpe ratio of 0.109. Levy and Roll (2018) employ shrinkage assuming that the standard deviation is known and that the return distribution is stable over time. This corresponds to the case $(\gamma_\mu = \frac{1}{2}, \gamma_\sigma = 1)$, i.e. the point at the top center of the figure, and yields a slightly higher out-of-sample Sharpe ratio of 0.115. We find that the

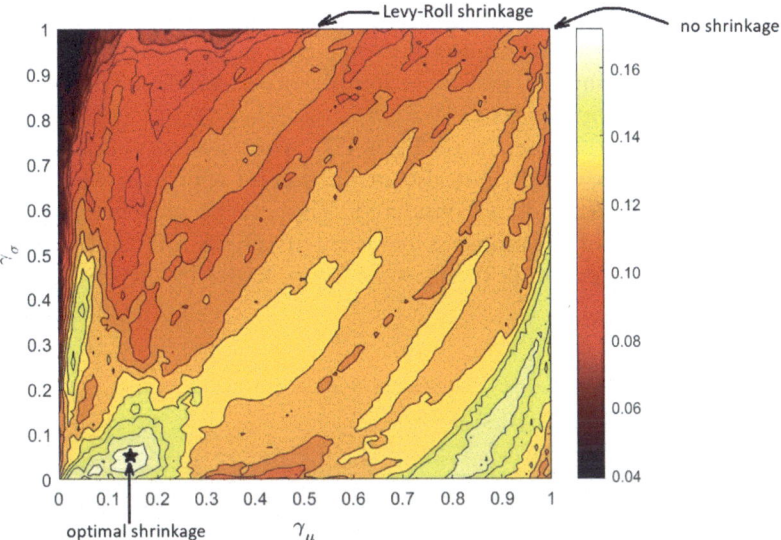

Fig. 4.4 The out-of-sample Sharpe ratio of the top 10 funds with the highest SAS, as a function of the shrinkage intensities, γ_μ and γ_σ. Lighter colors (shades) indicate better performance, as shown by the vertical color-bar legend to the right of the figure. The best out-of-sample performance is obtained with the combination $\gamma_\mu - 0.15$ and $\gamma_\sigma - 0.04$, denoted by the star. This shrinkage yields an out-of-sample Sharpe ratio of 0.169, which is higher not only of that obtained by ranking according to the standard sample Sharpe (0.109, top right corner), and Levy and Roll (2018) shrinkage (0.115, top center), but it is also higher than the Sharpe ratio of the market portfolio over the same period, which is 0.148

combination that yields the highest Sharpe ratio is:

$$\gamma_\mu = 0.15, \quad \gamma_\sigma = 0.04, \tag{4.7}$$

denoted by the star in the figure. This combination yields an out-of-sample Sharpe ratio of 0.169. This is not only much higher compared to the cases of no shrinkage or the Levy and Roll (2018) shrinkage, but it is even higher than the Sharpe ratio of the market portfolio over the corresponding period, which is 0.148. This difference in the Sharpe ratios corresponds to an annual risk-adjusted excess return of about 1.1% relative to the market,[4] and implies not only that some funds are able to beat the market, but also that these funds can be identified *ex-ante* and exploited by employing SAS.

The shrinkage parameters of Eq. (4.7) work well not only when considering the top funds, but also in the second approach, where the performance of *all* funds is considered. This can be seen in Fig. 4.5, which describes the relationship between in-sample SAS and out-of-sample Sharpe ratios for all funds, sorted into deciles by their in-sample SAS.

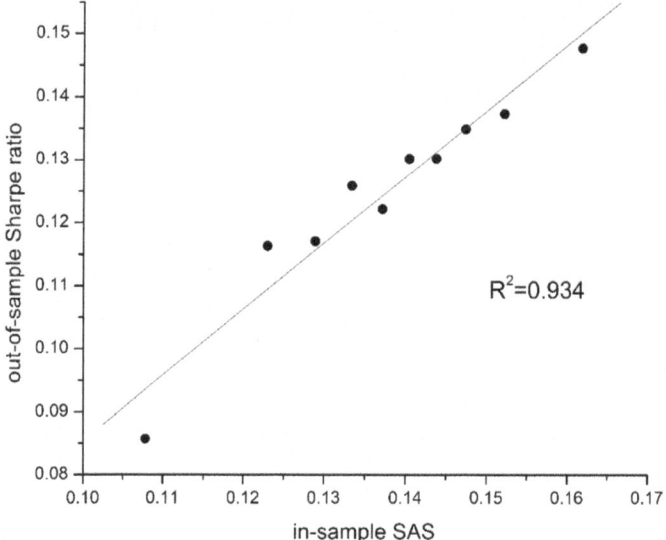

Fig. 4.5 Funds are sorted into deciles by their in-sample SAS. The equal-weighted average out-of-sample Sharpe ratio is shown as a function of the average in-sample SAS. The out-of-sample performance is almost monotonic in the in-sample SAS, and the linear fit is close to perfect, with $R^2 = 0.934$

[4] The S&P's monthly standard deviation is 4.46% in our sample period. Thus, the difference of $0.169 - 0.148 = 0.021$ in Sharpe ratios translates to a monthly risk-adjusted return difference of $0.021 \cdot 4.46\% = 0.094\%$, and to an annual risk-adjusted excess return of (approximately) $0.094 \cdot 12 = 1.13\%$.

Shrinking the sample gross returns but not the fees implies that the fees are weighed more heavily than the sample returns. How much over-weighing does $\gamma_\mu = 0.15$ imply? For a typical fund with $\hat{\sigma}_i = 4\%$, $\gamma_\mu = 0.15$ implies $\gamma_i = 0.2.$[5] This indicates that the weight of fees in the SAS is 5 times larger than that of the sample return [see Eq. (4.6)]. In other words, for two funds with the same volatility, a 5 basis-point difference in the sample average returns is required to compensate for a 1 basis-point difference in fees. Going back to the example in the Sect. 4.3, $\gamma_i = 0.2$ implies that fund B, with fees that are higher by 1% than those of fund A, should be preferred to fund A only if its sample gross return is 5% higher, i.e. only if its gross return is 16% or higher.[6] This implies a very substantial overweighing of fees, and reflects the large errors involved in estimating mean returns.

It is well-known that the estimation problem is typically more severe for mean returns than it is for standard deviations. It may thus seem surprising at first that the optimal out-of-sample performance is obtained with such a small value of $\gamma_\sigma = 0.04$. However, note that γ_σ determines not only the shrinkage of the sample $\hat{\sigma}$ toward the cross-sectional average, $\bar{\sigma}$, but also the importance of the sample standard deviation relative to the fees. To illustrate this point, consider the simplified case of $\gamma_\mu = 0$, where the SAS becomes $\frac{\overline{R}_i^{gross} - fee_i}{\gamma_\sigma \hat{\sigma}_i + (1 - \gamma_\sigma)\bar{\sigma}}$. The higher the value of γ_σ, the larger the variation in the denominator, and the more dominant the role of $\hat{\sigma}_i$ relative to fee_i. The fact that the optimal performance is obtained with very low values of γ_σ indicates that the role of the fees in predicting out-of-sample performance is much more pronounced than the role of the sample standard deviations. This is consistent with previous research suggesting that fees may be the best predictors of future performance (Carhart, 1997; Kinnel, 2010). This does not signify, however, that the sample return parameters should be ignored—as evident from the fact that the maximal out-of-sample performance is obtained with non-zero values of γ_μ and γ_σ.

---

[5] This is based on Eq. (4.4). σ_μ, the standard deviation of average returns across funds, is empirically about 0.6% (this value changes somewhat from one month to another). Thus, for $T = 60$ Eq. (4.4) becomes: $\gamma_i = \dfrac{1}{1 + \frac{4^2}{60 \cdot 0.6^2}\left(\frac{1}{0.15} - 1\right)} \cong 0.2$.

[6] $0.2 \cdot 11 - 1 = 0.2 \cdot 16 - 2$.

To get a better idea about the difference in rankings between SAS and the standard sample Sharpe ratio, let us look at the top 10 funds identified by these two measures. Table 4.1 provides these top funds, as of September 2016, with sample parameters based on the preceding 60 months. The table reports the in-sample average gross return and standard deviation for each fund, its fees, as well as its out-of-sample Sharpe ratio (net of fees) in the period October 2016–September 2021. The in-sample parameters reflect the (only) parameters observed by an investor starting to invest in September 2016. The out-of-sample Sharpe ratios are the unobservable "future" Sharpe ratios from the perspective of an investor making his investment decision in September 2016. The most obvious difference between these two groups of funds is the fees: the average (monthly) fees are 0.068% for the top Sharpe funds, compared to only 0.028% for the top SAS funds. This follows directly from the overweighting of fees implied by SAS. Because of the very small weight attached to the sample variance, SAS funds have higher sample volatilities than the Sharpe funds. As higher volatility funds tend to also have higher average returns, this relaxed constraint on the volatility also allows SAS funds to have higher sample returns. The average out-of-sample Sharpe ratio is 39.6% higher for the SAS funds: 0.261 compared to 0.187.[7] Moreover, if funds are ranked by their out-of-sample Sharpe ratios, each SAS fund has a higher Sharpe ratio than its counterpart Sharpe fund (this is analogous to the First-order Stochastic Dominance of one distribution over another, see Hadar & Russell, 1969, and Hanoch & Levy, 1969).

4.6   Robustness

The combination $\gamma_\mu = 0.15$, $\gamma_\sigma = 0.04$ [Eq. (4.7)] is found to yield the best out-of-sample performance when domestic equity funds and the 1991–2021 sample period are employed. If we are to employ these parameters when ranking funds *today*, we would feel more confident if we could be convinced that these optimal parameter values are not specific to these conditions. In order to examine the robustness of the out-of-sample performance of SAS with the shrinkage parameters in Eq. (4.7), we employ several different settings. First, we look at

---

[7] Note that these values are different than those reported in Fig. 4.5, which employs the entire sample period, compared to the September 2016 "snapshot" analysis reported here.

Table 4.1 The top 10 funds by in-sample Sharpe ratio (panel A) and by in-sample SAS (panel B), as of September 2016

rank	Fund i.d	Fund name	$\overline{R}_i^{\text{gross}}$	$\hat{\sigma}_i$	fee_i	Out-of-sample Sharpe ratio
(A) Top Funds by Sample Sharpe Ratio						
1	49,277	Fidelity Advisor Real Estate Class I	0.98	1.74	0.064	0.154
2	12,006	Fidelity Real Estate Income Fund	0.97	1.74	0.068	0.154
3	49,275	Fidelity Advisor Real Estate Class A	0.97	1.73	0.086	0.149
4	49,278	Fidelity Advisor Real Estate Class T	0.97	1.73	0.089	0.148
5	24,710	PowerShares High Yield Equity	1.44	2.93	0.045	0.162
6	49,276	Fidelity Advisor Real Estate Class C	0.96	1.72	0.148	0.133
7	43,925	US Managed Volatility	1.22	2.60	0.020	0.218
8	36,082	PIMCO StocksPLUS Long Duration	1.83	3.91	0.049	0.340
9	27,507	SEI Institutional Managed Trust	1.24	2.58	0.085	0.205
10	51,184	PowerShares KBW	1.58	3.48	0.029	0.210
		Average:	1.22	2.42	0.068	0.187
(B) Top Funds by Sample SAS						
1	31,366	Vanguard Health Care Admiral Class	1.54	3.61	0.008	0.304
2	31,357	Vanguard Health Care ETF Class Shares	1.54	3.61	0.008	0.304
3	36,082	PIMCO StocksPLUS Long Duration	1.83	3.91	0.049	0.340

(continued)

Table 4.1 (continued)

rank	Fund i.d	Fund name	$\overline{R}_i^{\text{gross}}$	$\hat{\sigma}_i$	fee_i	Out-of-sample Sharpe ratio
4	51,184	PowerShares KBW	1.58	3.48	0.029	0.210
5	24,710	PowerShares High Yield Equity	1.44	2.93	0.045	0.162
6	27,428	PowerShares S&P 500 Quality	1.58	3.67	0.033	0.279
7	16,463	iShares US Healthcare	1.54	3.53	0.037	0.299
8	49,219	PowerShares S&P SmallCap	1.47	3.64	0.024	0.172
9	43,925	US Managed Volatility Fund; Class A Shares	1.22	2.60	0.020	0.218
10	24,748	PowerShares S&P 500 Quality	1.30	2.95	0.024	0.318
		Average:	1.51	3.39	0.028	0.261

Return parameters are monthly, in %, and are estimated from the previous $T = 60$ months. The out-of-sample Sharpe ratio is net of fees

additional fund classes. We separately examine foreign equity funds and fixed-income funds. Second, we split the sample period and look at the performance of domestic equity funds in the two subperiods: 1991–2006 and 2006–2021. Finally, we examine robustness relative to the length of the estimation window, T.

Different Asset Classes

Our main analysis is conducted on U.S. domestic equity funds. How well do the parameters in Eq. (4.7) perform when applied to other mutual fund classes? Fig. 4.6 shows the out-of-sample Sharpe ratio of the top 10 SAS funds for different $(\gamma_\mu, \gamma_\sigma)$ combinations, for foreign equity funds (panel A), and fixed-income funds (corporate and municipal bonds, panel B). The star depicts the parameter values in Eq. (4.7), i.e. those that were found to be optimal for domestic equity funds. For each asset class, the highest out-of-sample performance is obtained at different $(\gamma_\mu, \gamma_\sigma)$

combinations, but the parameters in Eq. (4.7) yield good out-of-sample performance for both foreign equity funds and fixed-income funds. In both cases, SAS with these parameters yields superior performance relative to both the standard sample Sharpe ratio and the Levy and Roll (2018) Shrinkage. In the case of foreign equity funds, SAS yields an out-of-sample Sharpe ratio of 0.154, compared to 0.137 of the standard Sharpe ranking (top right corner), and 0.136 of Levy-Roll shrinkage (top center). For fixed-income funds, SAS yields an out-of-sample Sharpe ratio of 0.151, compared to 0.048 of the standard Sharpe ranking, and 0.066 of the Levy-Roll shrinkage.

Figure 4.7 reports the relationship between in-sample performance and out-of-sample performance for *all* funds in each asset class (rather than just the top 10 funds, as in Fig. 4.6). In both cases, in-sample SAS provides higher explanatory power than the standard Sharpe ratio.

Different Sample Periods

To examine the consistency of the results over time, we divide the sample period into two subperiods, and analyze each subperiod separately. The first subperiod is December 1991–October 2006 and the second November 2006–September 2021. Figures 4.8 and 4.9 report the results—Fig. 4.8 for the top 10 domestic equity funds, and Fig. 4.9 for all domestic equity funds. In both subperiods, the shrinkage parameters in Eq. (4.7) (denoted by the star) peform well, and are better than both the standard Sharpe ratio (no shrinkage), and the Levy and Roll (2018) shrinkage. In the first subperiod, the top 10 SAS funds yield an out-of-sample Sharpe ratio of 0.198, compared to 0.137 for the top 10 in-sample Sharpe funds, and 0.132 for Levy and Roll (2018) shrinkage. In the second subperiod, the top SAS funds yield an out-of-sample Sharpe ratio of 0.142, compared to 0.127 for the top in-sample Sharpe funds, and 0.115 for Levy and Roll (2018) shrinkage.

A Shorter Estimation Window

The formula for γ_i takes the number of observations, T, into account, see Eq. (4.3–4.4). Thus, we do not expect the optimal γ_μ to be very sensitive to the choice of the length of the estimation window, T. The optimal γ_σ could potentially depend on T, but its value is very small anyway ($\gamma_\sigma = 0.04$), implying that the sample standard deviations are

Fig. 4.6 The out-of-sample Sharpe ratio of the top 10 funds with highest SAS, as a function of the shrinkage intensities, γ_μ and γ_σ. Panel A: foreign equity funds. Panel B: corporate and municipal bond funds. The star represents the shrinkage which was found to be optimal for domestic equity funds: $\gamma_\mu = 0.15$, $\gamma_\sigma = 0.04$. In both cases, this shrinkage is close to optimal, and yields out-of-sample performance superior to both the standard sample Sharpe ratio (top right corner: $\gamma_\mu = 1$, $\gamma_\sigma = 1$) and to Levy and Roll (2018) shrinkage (top center: $\gamma_\mu = \frac{1}{2}$, $\gamma_\sigma = 1$)

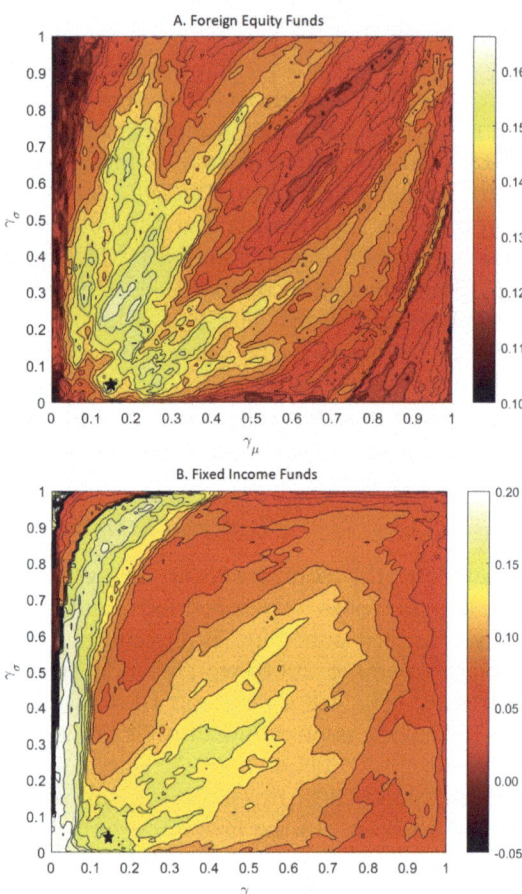

almost ignored. In the preceding analysis, we employ $T = 60$ months (5 years), which is standard practice in many applications. Another popular alternative is the choice of $T = 36$ months, i.e. 3 years. Figure 4.10 shows the results for this case. While the optimal out-of-sample performance is obtained at a slightly lower value of γ_μ ($\gamma_\mu = 0.1$, $\gamma_\sigma = 0.05$), these parameter values are very close to those in Eq. (4.7). The parameters in Eq. (4.7), denoted in the figure by the star, yield an out-of-sample Sharpe ratio of 0.197, which is almost maximal, and it is much higher than the

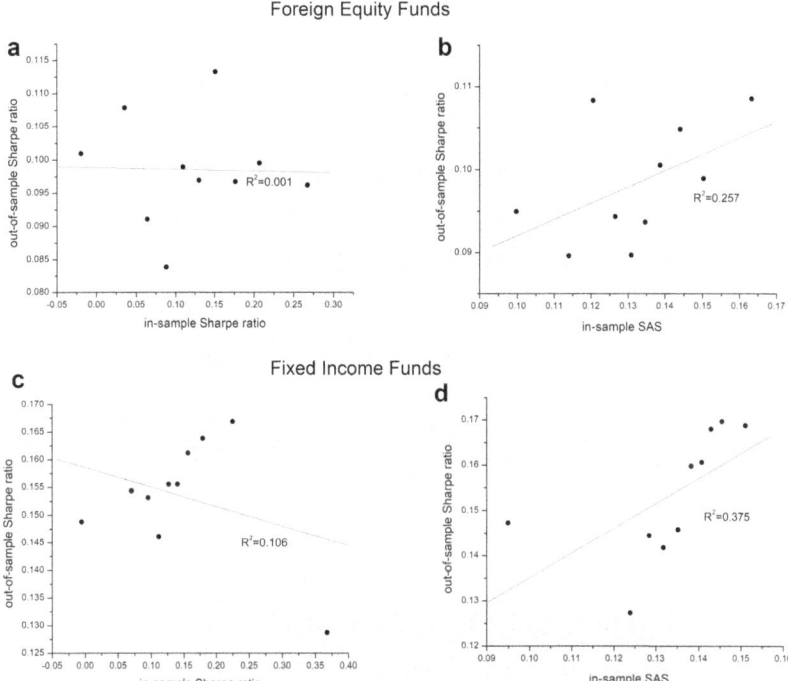

Fig. 4.7 The relationship between in-sample performance and the out-of-sample Sharpe ratio for all funds in each asset class. All funds are sorted into deciles according to the in-sample performance. Panel A: foreign equity funds, the standard sample Sharpe ratio is employed as the in-sample performance measure. Panel B: foreign equity funds, SAS [with parameters in Eq. (4.7)] is employed as the in-sample performance measure. Panel C: corporate and municipal bond funds, the standard Sharpe ratio is employed as the in-sample performance measure. Panel D: corporate and municipal bond funds, SAS is employed as the in-sample performance measure

one obtained with the standard Sharpe ratio (0.109), or the Levy and Roll (2018) shrinkage (0.115).

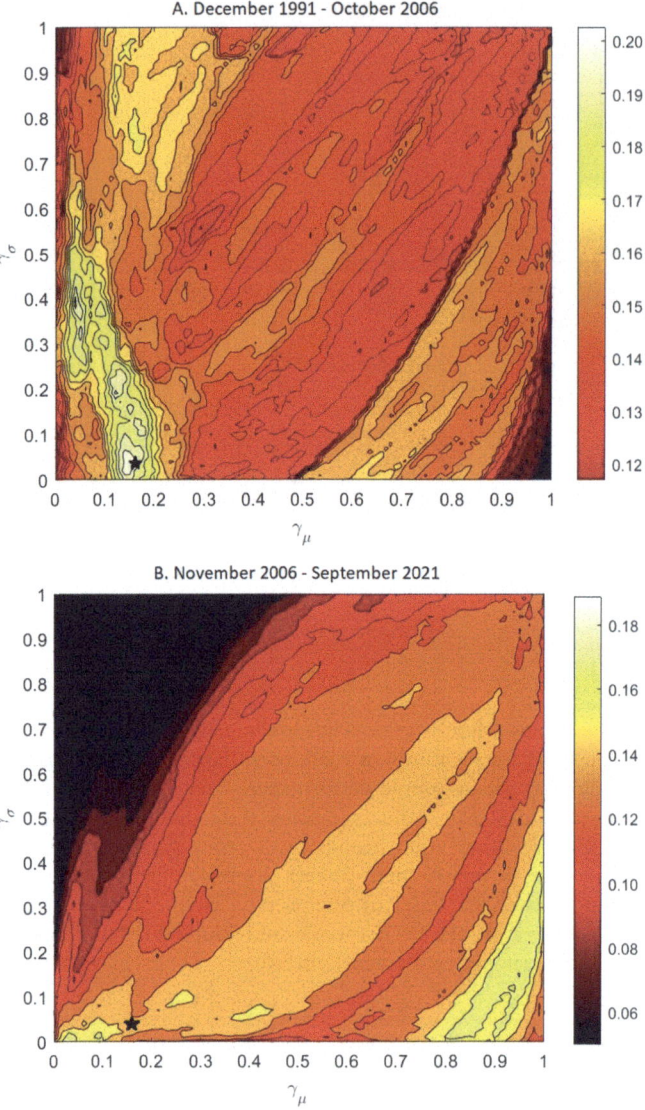

Fig. 4.8 The out-of-sample Sharpe ratio of the top 10 funds with highest sample SAS, as a function of the shrinkage intensities, γ_μ and γ_σ, for two subperiods. Panel A: December 1991–October 2006. Panel B: November 2006–September 2021. The star represents the shrinkage parameters in Eq. (4.7): $\gamma_\mu = 0.15$, $\gamma_\sigma = 0.04$. In both subperiods, this shrinkage is close to optimal, and yields out-of-sample performance superior to both the standard sample Sharpe ratio and to Levy and Roll (2018) shrinkage

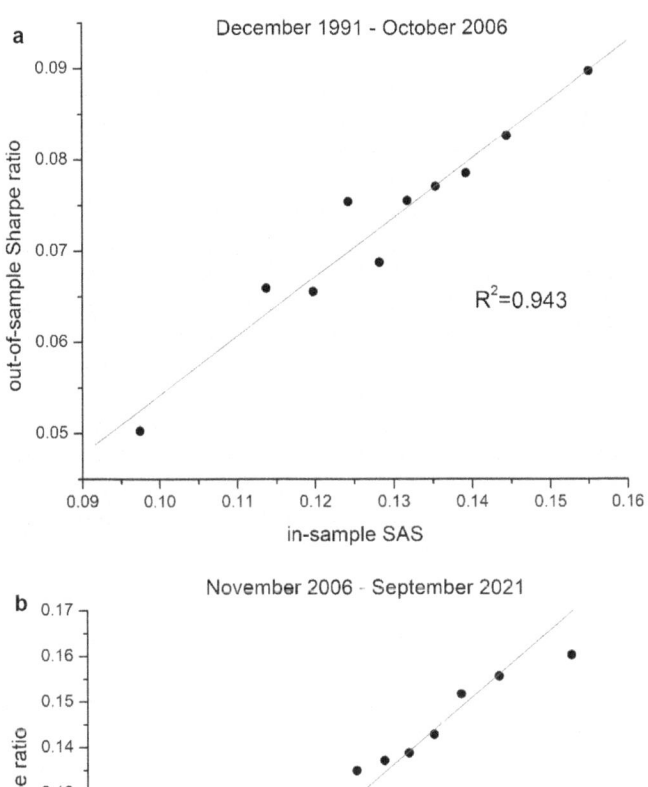

Fig. 4.9 The relationship between in-sample performance and the out-of-sample Sharpe ratio for all domestic equity funds, in two subperiods. Funds are sorted into deciles according to in-sample SAS with the parameters in Eq. (4.7)

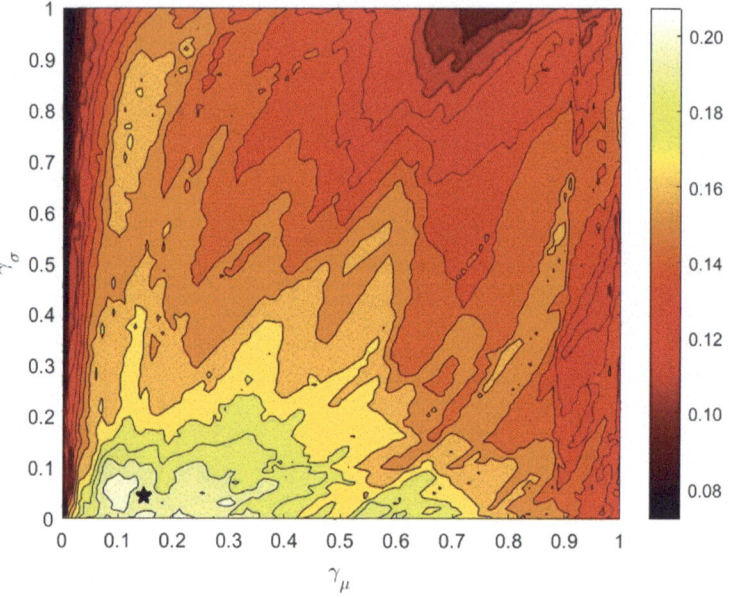

Fig. 4.10 The out-of-sample Sharpe ratio of the top 10 domestic equity funds with highest sample SAS, as a function of the shrinkage intensities, γ_μ and γ_σ, when the estimation window length is $T = 36$ months. The star represents the optimal parameters obtained with $T = 60$ months (Eq. (4.7): $\gamma_\mu = 0.15$, $\gamma_\sigma = 0.04$)

4.7   SUMMARY

Estimating the future return parameters is a messy business: past returns provide very noisy information about future returns. As a consequence, the relation between past parameters and future parameters is very weak. This is true for average returns, alphas, Morningstar ratings, as well as for Sharpe ratios. Rankings based on the past (i.e. sample) parameters have almost no predictive ability regarding future performance. This paints a very troubling picture: it implies that the trillions of dollars invested in mutual funds are invested almost blindly. This is a problem not only for investors, but also for the economy as a whole, as it implies a macroeconomic inefficiency in the allocation of capital to firms.

Fund ranking can be substantially improved by employing two techniques: statistical shrinkage, and treatment of fees separately from returns. Since fees are much less noisy than returns, they should be given more weight in a predictor. The Shrinkage-Adjusted Sharpe Ratio (SAS) implements these ideas and provides a substantial improvement in out-of-sample performance. Empirically, we find that fees should be typically weighed roughly 5 times more than the historical returns. This means that a 5 basis-point difference in the historical average returns of two funds is required to compensate for a 1 basis-point difference in fees.

The performance of the SAS is shown here to be robust across different asset classes, sample periods, and estimation window lengths. Clearly, there is still a great deal of noise in ranking: choosing the fund with the highest sample SAS does not guarantee that this fund will do well in the future. Chance plays an unavoidably central role in investments, as further discussed in Chapter 7. However, given this fundamental limitation, SAS offers a welcome improvement relative to existing methods. We hope it will be adopted by investors and rating agencies as a guide for fund selection.

References

Bollen, N. P., & Busse, J. A. (2001). On the timing ability of mutual fund managers. *The Journal of Finance, 56*(3), 1075–1094.

Carhart, M. M. (1997). On persistence in mutual fund performance. *The Journal of Finance, 52*(1), 57–82.

Gruber, M. J. (1996). Another puzzle: The growth in actively managed mutual funds. *The Journal of Finance, 51*(3), 783–810.

Hadar, J., & Russell, W. R. (1969). Rules for ordering uncertain prospects. *The American Economic Review, 59*(1), 25–34.

Hanoch, G., & Levy, H. (1969). The efficiency analysis of choices involving risk. *Review of Economic Studies, 36*(3), 335–346.

James, W., & Stein, C. (1961). Estimation with quadratic loss. In *Proceedings of the 4th Berkeley symposium on mathematical statistics and probability, volume 1: Contributions to the theory of statistics*.

Jorion, P. (1986). Bayes-Stein estimation for portfolio analysis. *Journal of Financial and Quantitative Analysis, 21*(3), 279–292.

Kinnel, R. (2010). *How expense ratios and star ratings predict success.* https://www.morningstar.com/articles/347327/article

Lee, P. M. (2012). *Bayesian statistics.* Oxford University Press.

Levi, Y., & Welch, I. (2017). Best practice for cost-of-capital estimates. *Journal of Financial and Quantitative Analysis, 52*(2), 427–463.

Levy, M., & Roll, R. (2018). Generalized performance measures: Optimal overweighing of fees relative to sample returns. *The Journal of Portfolio Management, 44*(3), 66–75.

Levy, M., & Roll, R. (2023). The shrinkage adjusted sharpe ratio: An improved method for mutual fund selection. *The Journal of Investing, 32*(2), 7–23.

Lo, A. W. (2002). The statistics of Sharpe ratios. *Financial Analysts Journal, 58*(4), 36–52.

Philips, C. B., Kinniry Jr, F. M. (2010). *Mutual fund ratings and future performance*. Vanguard Group, 20.

Vasicek, O. A. (1973). A note on using cross-sectional information in Bayesian estimation of security betas. *The Journal of Finance, 28*(5), 1233–1239.

Zheng, L. (1999). Is money smart? A study of mutual fund investors' fund selection ability. *The Journal of Finance, 54*(3), 901–933.

CHAPTER 5

Active Versus Passive Investment

Abstract About 92% of active mutual funds underperform the S&P500
index. Moreover, the persistence of fund performance over time is very
weak, making it difficult to identify in advance the minority of active funds
that will beat the index in the future. The annual aggregate loss due to
active investing is estimated at $235 billion. This loss can be decomposed
into an inefficient portfolio composition component of $186 billion and a
$49 billion component, which is a wealth transfer from investors to funds
as fees.

Keywords Active management · Passive management · Market index ·
Management fees · Sharpe ratio · Deadweight loss

Active investors believe that they can identify stocks that are underpriced
(or overpriced), and that by buying (or shorting) them, they can achieve
"abnormal returns", which basically means beating a market portfolio
(e.g. the S&P 500 index). Active investors collect and analyze information
to identify lucrative investment opportunities. Therefore, active investment strategies are relatively expensive. Active mutual funds are funds
that employ an active investment strategy.

In contrast, passive investors believe that mispricing, to the extent it
exists, is not large enough to justify the expense required to find it.

© The Author(s), under exclusive license to Springer Nature   79
Switzerland AG 2024
M. Levy and R. Roll, *Mutual Fund Selection*,
https://doi.org/10.1007/978-3-031-69758-6_5

Passive investors simply buy a "market portfolio" that holds every available stock, each with a weight proportional to its market capitalization. In practical terms, the S&P 500 index serves as an excellent proxy for the entire U.S. "market portfolio" of all stocks.[1] Similarly, the FTSE, DAX, Nikkei, and TA 125 indexes are proxies for the market portfolios of the U.K., Germany, Japan, and Israel, respectively. Passive mutual funds follow a passive investment strategy. Passive investing is called "passive" not only because it does not require any information gathering and processing, but also because it does not entail much trading.[2] Consequently, fees of passive funds are typically much lower than those of active funds.[3] The underlying rationale of passive investing is related to the concept of "the wisdom of the crowd": while individuals may have quite inaccurate estimations about the "correct price" of a stock, the market price aggregates all these estimations, and therefore represents a weighted average of all investors' opinions. It turns out that in many contexts, it is difficult for any individual expert to beat the average opinion of the crowd.[4] The Capital Asset Pricing Model (CAPM) reflects this idea—one of the model's two dramatic predictions is that the market portfolio is the optimal tangency portfolio. According to the CAPM, no other portfolio yields a Sharpe ratio greater than the market's.

---

[1] The theoretical market portfolio includes all stocks in the market. There are thousands of stocks traded in the U.S. market. In contrast, the S&P 500 index includes only the 500 largest stocks. Thus, it may seem that these two portfolios are very different. However, the 500 largest stocks account for more than 90% of the total aggregate market value, so that the return on the S&P 500 is very close to the return of the theoretical market portfolio.

[2] Consider, for example, an alternative "naïve" strategy of investing equal amounts in all assets. This strategy does not require information processing, but it does require constant trading. If the price of stock A goes up and the price of stock B goes down, one needs to sell shares of stock A and buy shares of stock B to maintain equal holdings. In contrast, once one buys the market index, no further trading is required: price changes affect the weights in the market portfolio and in the investor's portfolio in exactly the same way. Thus, a passive fund tracking the S&P 500 index, for example, needs to trade only in response to net flows to the fund, and on occasion, in response to changes in the constituents of the S&P 500 index.

[3] For example, in 2023, the annual fee on the Vanguard S&P 500 ETF was only 0.03%. In contrast, typical annual fees in active funds are in the order of 1%.

[4] Galton (1907) reports one of the most famous examples of this concept. In a 1906 country fair, 800 people participated in a contest of estimating the weight of an ox. Galton observed that the median guess, 1207 pounds, was accurate within 1% of the true weight of 1198 pounds. See Surowiecki (2005) for many other examples.

In equilibrium, the active and passive strategies can, and indeed are expected to, co-exist. Roll (1994) explains this co-existence by an analogy to the "hawk-dove" model from evolutionary biology:

> Investors compete for the most "undervalued" asset. The hawk strategy is conducting security analysis. The dove strategy is passive investing: expending no effort on information analysis. Clearly, if everyone analyses securities, the benefits will be less than the costs. If everyone is passive, the benefits of analysis will be tremendous. The equilibrium is that some analyze, some don't... the final equilibrium is characterized by a situation in which it is not worthwhile for the marginal passive investor to begin analyzing nor for the marginal active investor to cease conducting security analysis. (Roll, 1994, p. 72).

In equilibrium, both strategies are expected to yield the same risk-adjusted performance after fees: talented active managers will extract the surplus they produce as fees, and investors will thus be indifferent between active and passive funds (Berk & Green, 2004). Is the market in such an equilibrium? Do active and passive strategies yield the same performance after fees? In this chapter, we will examine these questions empirically.

5.1 METHODS

In line with the conclusions of Chapters 2 and 3, and following Levy (2023), a fund's performance can be measured by its Sharpe ratio, net of fees. We examine this ratio for all active U.S. funds, and thereby compare each fund's performance to that of the passive strategy of holding the market portfolio, which is approximated by the S&P500 index (including dividends). A fund with a Sharpe ratio greater than the market's is considered over-performing, and one with a Sharpe ratio lower than the market's is underperforming. We define fund i's risk-adjusted excess return, Δ_i, as the difference between the fund's actual average return and the hypothetical mean return that would have equated the fund's Sharpe ratio with that of the market.

The hypothetical mean return $\overline{R}_i^*$ that equates the Sharpe ratio of fund i with that of the market is obtained from:

$$\frac{\overline{R}_i^* - r_{\mathrm{f}}}{\sigma_i} = \frac{\overline{R}_M - r_{\mathrm{f}}}{\sigma_M}, \tag{5.1}$$

where σ_i denotes the fund's standard deviation, r_f is the risk-free rate, and $\overline{R}_M$ and σ_M are the market portfolio's expected return and standard deviation, respectively. Thus,

$$\overline{R}_i^* = \frac{\sigma_i}{\sigma_M}\left(\overline{R}_M - r_f\right) + r_f. \tag{5.2}$$

Δ_i is the difference between the fund's *actual* average return, $\overline{R}_i$, and the above hypothetical $\overline{R}_i^*$, i.e.:

$$\Delta_i \equiv \overline{R}_i - \overline{R}_i^* = \overline{R}_i - \frac{\sigma_i}{\sigma_M}\left(\overline{R}_M - r_f\right) - r_f. \tag{5.3}$$

Figure 5.1 illustrates the geometric interpretation of Δ_i. Note that Δ is somewhat analogous to Jensen's α in the sense that both measure a vertical distance from a straight line originating in r_f (compare Figs. 5.1, 5.2, 5.3). The difference is that Jensen's α takes beta as the measure of risk, and measures the vertical distance from the SML, while Δ is based on the standard deviation as the measure of risk, and measures the fund's vertical distance from the Capital Market Line (CML). A positive Δ implies that the fund is above the CML, i.e. it outperforms the market. A negative Δ, as in the case shown in Fig. 5.1, implies that the fund is below the CML, meaning that it underperforms relative to the market.

Below we report the average Δ, and other distributional properties of Δ across all active funds. Δ is an excess return and is measured in percentage terms. To estimate the risk-adjusted dollar value created/destroyed by a fund, we multiply its Δ by its size, measured as its total net asset value; i.e.[5]

$$VA_i = \Delta_i \cdot TNA_i. \tag{5.4}$$

The total VA_i aggregated across all funds is the total risk-adjusted value created/destroyed by the active mutual fund industry.

Passive index funds are excluded from the analysis because their Sharpe ratios should, theoretically, be the same as their benchmark's ratios, by

---

[5] This is in the spirit of Berk and van Binsbergen (2015), but since we are interested in investors' welfare, rather than in managers' talent, we employ the Sharpe ratio rather than alpha, and we look at returns net of fees. These differences have a huge impact on the estimated aggregate loss by the active mutual fund industry, as discussed below.

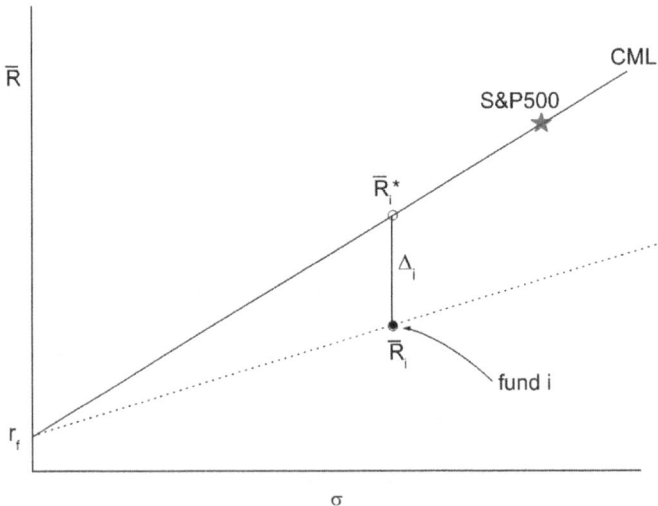

Fig. 5.1 Fund i's risk-adjusted excess return, Δ_i, is measured as the difference between the fund's actual average return, $\overline{R}_i$, and the hypothetical average return it should have in order to equate its Sharpe with that of the S&P500 index, $\overline{R}_i^*$ [Eq. (5.3)]. A positive Δ_i implies over-performance (the fund is above the CML), and a negative Δ_i implies underperformance (the fund is below the CML, as shown in the figure)

construction.[6] Monthly data for total fund assets and fees are mostly unavailable before December 1991, thus, we take the sample period of December 1991–March 2021 (352 months). The market portfolio is taken as the S&P 500 index, including dividends (CRSP S&P 500 value-weighted series including distributions). Monthly risk-free rates are taken from the CRSP Monthly Risk-free Series.

5.2 RESULTS

Figure 5.2 plots all active domestic equity funds on the mean-volatility plane. The monthly average return and standard deviation are estimated by employing the 120-month period of April 2011–March 2021. Each

---

[6] For some passive funds, this is not exactly the case because they outperform their benchmarks slightly by lending securities and/or engaging in astute trading.

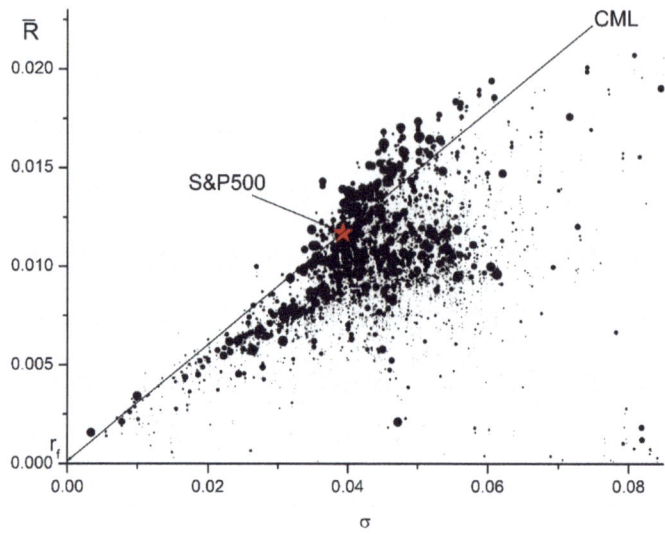

Fig. 5.2 A mean-volatility picture of the mutual fund industry. All active U.S. domestic equity funds with complete return records over the April 2011–March 2021 are shown. The average monthly return and standard deviation are estimated for this sample period. Each fund is depicted by a circle, the area of which is proportional to its size (total net assets as of March 2021).[7] The figure reveals that most funds (92.1%) underperform relative to the S&P500 index. The relationship between size and performance is weak (a correlation of 0.098)

fund is depicted by a circle with an area that is proportional to its size (total net assets, as of March 2021). The figure conveys two main messages: First, most funds in this sample (92.1%) underperform relative to the passive market index, i.e. they are below the straight line connecting the market with the risk-free asset (the CML). Second, there does not seem to be a strong association between size and performance. Indeed, the correlation between funds' Sharpe ratios and size is only 0.098. This low correlation is consistent with the equilibrium viewpoint

[7] The fact that we are measuring fund size by the assets at the *end* of the period introduces a slight bias: funds that have done well tend to be larger at the end of the period. However, note that fund sizes span a huge scale: the largest fund is about 2,600 times larger than the median fund (Levy 2023). Thus, the bias implied by the differences in performance is negligible relative to the underlying differences in size.

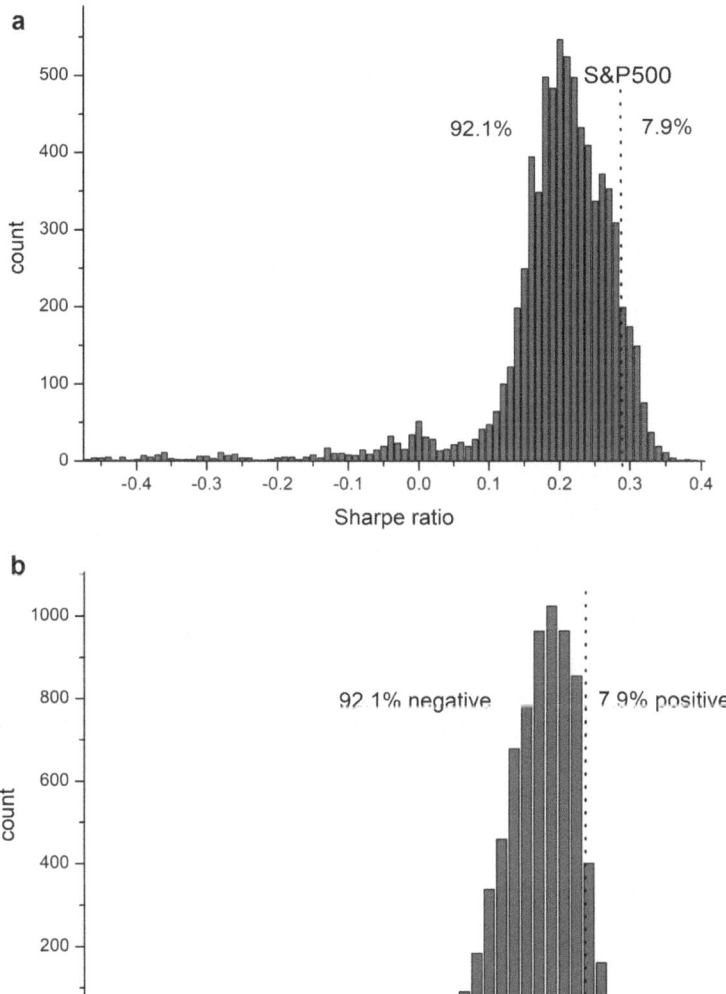

Fig. 5.3 The distribution of Sharpe ratios (Panel A) and Δ's (Panel B). 7.9% of funds over-perform relative to the S&P500 index, and 92.1% underperform

of Berk and Green (2004), by which talented managers attract investment flows up to the point where the amount of money they manage depresses net-of-fees performance back to "normal" levels. Alternatively, this low correlation could also be driven by the notorious difficulty of predicting future performance, as discussed in Chapter 4.

Figure 5.3 shows the distribution of funds' Sharpe ratios (Panel A), and their Δ's, as defined by Eq. (5.3), (Panel B). The figure shows that in this period, only 7.9% of the funds over-perform relative to the S&P 500 index, while the other 92.1% underperform. Moreover, over-performance, when it exists, is typically moderate. In contrast, underperformance can be spectacular. For the April 2011–March 2021 sample period employed here, the Sharpe ratio of the S&P 500 index is 0.288; the mean Sharpe ratio of active funds is 0.192, and the median is 0.207; the maximal Sharpe ratio across all funds is 0.392, and the minimal Sharpe ratio is -0.475. The average monthly Δ, equal-weighted across all fund, Δ_{EW} is -0.54%, and the value-weighted average monthly Δ, Δ_{VW}, is -0.20%. These monthly measures correspond to an annual underperformance of roughly 6.5% and 2.4%, respectively.

One could argue that the comparison of all equity funds with market index is unfair, because some of the funds included in this category are balanced funds, that are mandated to hold a minimum allocation in bonds. If bonds have performed poorly, this may drive some of the under-performance. In order to examine this issue, we analyzed the performance of bond funds over the same time period. On average, bond funds had an average monthly return of 0.33% and a standard deviation of 1.15%, compared to an average return of 0.94% and a standard deviation of 4.73% for equity funds. In terms of Sharpe ratios, bond funds did better, not worse, than equity funds: their average Sharpe ratio is 0.245, compared to 0.192 of equity funds.[8] Thus, it seems that an exogeneous constraint on the minimal allocation to bonds cannot explain the underperformance of balanced funds relative to the index.

Figures 5.2 and 5.3 paint a rather bleak picture of the active mutual fund industry. As the vast majority of funds underperform passive investment in the market, this industry on the aggregate induces a loss to investors. To estimate this aggregate loss, we employ Eq. (5.4) for each

---

[8] It turns out that this situation is not a-typical: in the 120 months preceding our sample period, bond funds had an average Sharpe ratio of 0.126, while the average Sharpe ratio of equity funds was 0.072.

fund, and aggregate across all funds. The annual aggregate loss is obtained by multiplying the monthly *VA* by 12.[9] We find that the aggregate annual loss induced by active funds is $223.9 billion. When we repeat the analysis, but use fund gross returns before fees, rather than the net returns, the annual loss is reduced to $180.4 billion. This means that $180.4 billion of the loss is due to an inefficient portfolio allocation or wealth destruction, and the rest, $43.5 billion, are fees transferred from investors to funds.

In the analysis above, 120 monthly returns are employed to estimate the funds' average returns and standard deviations. The estimates of the average Δ and the aggregate dollar loss are not very sensitive to the length of the estimation window. Table 5.1 shows the results for estimation windows of 36, 60, and 90 months (all ending in March 31, 2021). Panel A reports the results when the Sharpe ratio is employed, and the over-/underperformance is measured by Δ. The aggregate annual loss averaged over all specifications is $234.7 billion. The average aggregate loss before fees is $186.2 billion, and the difference, $48.5 billion is due to fees. Similar results are obtained when moving windows are employed to estimate the parameters, rather than windows ending in 2021 (see Levy 2023 for details).

Most of the literature on mutual fund performance employs alpha as the performance measure. Panels B and C report the results, when performance is measured by alpha, rather than the Sharpe ratio. In panel B, the Fama and French (1995) and Carhart (1997) 4-factor model is employed, and in panel C, the Fama and French (2015) 5-factor model is employed. The difference between the loss estimates obtained with alpha versus those obtained with the Sharpe ratio is dramatic: when the Sharpe ratio is employed, the loss is 6–15 times larger than when α's are employed. Chapter 2 shows that the Sharpe ratio is much better aligned with investors' welfare than alpha. Thus, we believe that the more severe results of panel A are the relevant ones. Also, note that in the CAPM

---

[9] An alternative way to obtain an estimate of the annual value created/destroyed from the monthly returns is to employ the multi-period mean and variance formulas of Tobin (1965) and Levhari and Levy (1977, Eq. 2):

$$1 + \mu_n = (1 + \mu_1)^{12} \quad \sigma_n^2 = \left(\sigma_1^2 + \mu_1^2\right)^n - \mu_1^{2n},$$ where μ_1 and σ_1^2 denote the 1-period

mean and variance, respectively, and μ_n and σ_n^2 denote the n-period parameters (these formulas employ the assumption of i.i.d returns). Both approaches yield similar results: the annual loss estimated by the formulas above is $236.5 billion, compared to the estimate of $223.9 billion obtained by the multiplication of the monthly loss by 12.

Table 5.1 Monthly parameters and aggregate annual loss for various estimation windows

Number of months in the estimation window	Δ_{EW}	Δ_{VW}	% of positive Δ's	Aggregate loss	Aggregate loss before fees
(A) Loss estimate based on Sharpe ratios					
36	− 0.49%	− 0.18%	17.7%	$258.9	$205.7
60	− 0.47%	− 0.15%	17.0%	$204.4	$153.9
90	− 0.54%	− 0.21%	9.4%	$251.4	$204.8
120	− 0.54%	− 0.20%	7.9%	$223.9	$180.4
Average:	− 0.51%	− 0.19%	13.0%	$234.7	$186.2

Number of months in the estimation window	α_{EW}	α_{VW}	% of positive α's	Aggregate loss	Aggregate loss before fees
(B) Loss estimate based on 4-factor α's					
36	− 0.14%	− 0.021%	27.3%	$29.7	− $23.4*
60	− 0.17%	− 0.037%	19.2%	$51.3	$0.7
90	− 0.17%	− 0.033%	16.5%	$40.0	− $6.5*
120	− 0.19%	− 0.039%	15.9%	$43.3	− $0.2*
Average:	− 0.17%	− 0.033%	19.7%	$41.1	− $7.4*

Number of months in the estimation window	α_{EW}	α_{VW}	% of positive α's	Aggregate loss	Aggregate loss before fees
(C) Loss Estimate Based on 5-Factor α's					
36	− 0.08%	0.022%	37.5%	− $31.5	− $84.6*
60	− 0.16%	− 0.028%	20.9%	$38.8	− $11.7*
90	− 0.16%	− 0.024%	18.1%	$29.3	− $17.3*
120	− 0.17%	− 0.025%	19.5%	$27.9	− $15.6*
Average:	− 0.14%	− 0.014%	24.0%	$16.1	− $32.3*

We consider estimation windows of different length, all ending in March 31, 2021. For each window length, we calculate the sample return parameters and Δ for each fund by Eq. (5.3) in the corresponding window. Δ_{EW} is the equal-weighted average Δ across all funds, and Δ_{VW} is the value-weighted average Δ. The monthly value created/destroyed by each fund is given by Eq. (5.4), and the annual value is obtained by multiplying the monthly value by 12. The aggregate annual loss is reported in billions of dollars, and is obtained by summing over all funds.
*A negative aggregate loss implies an aggregate gain.

framework, the value weighted average α of all assets is by definition zero. In contrast to the Sharpe ratio, a portfolio's α is simply the weighted average of the α's of the assets in the portfolio. Thus, in the CAPM setting, if all funds on aggregate hold the market, the weighted average α of all funds *should* be zero.

5.3   THE MAGNITUDE
OF THE AGGREGATE LOSS IN PERSPECTIVE

We estimate that the active mutual fund industry induces an aggregate annual loss of $234.7 billion. This figure can be decomposed into a $186.2 billion component, which is due to inefficient portfolio allocation relative to the passive market benchmark, and a $48.5 billion component, which is a wealth transfer from investors to funds, in the form of fees. This loss is very substantial. For comparison, it is 70% higher than the estimated deadweight loss of income taxation (Browning, 1976), and 23 times larger than the estimated deadweight loss of Christmas (Waldfogel, 1993).[10] It is interesting to compare the magnitude of the loss to a closely related issue that attracts a great deal of public attention—corporate managerial compensation. The top 200 CEOs in the U.S. receive an average compensation that is about 400 times larger than the average salary (Levy, 2016). While some view CEO compensation as an equilibrium outcome rewarding talent (Axelson & Bond, 2015; Cremers & Grinstein, 2014; Gabaix & Landier, 2008; Hubbard, 2005; Oyer, 2004; Tervio, 2008), others claim that a large part of this compensation does *not* constitute pay for performance and represents an economic inefficiency (Bebchuk & Fried, 2003, 2009; Bertrand & Mullainathan, 2001; Goergen & Renneboog, 2011; Levy, 2016; Newman & Mozes, 1999; Rappaport & Nodine, 1999). The total compensation of all S&P 500 firms' CEOs in 2022 was $8.4 billion.[11] Even if a large part of this compensation represents economic inefficiency, this inefficiency is dwarfed by the inefficiency of the active mutual fund industry, which is more than 20 times larger.

---

[10] Browning estimates the annual welfare cost of taxation at $19 billion in 1974 terms, which translate to $108 billion in 2021 terms (inflated using the CPI). Waldfogel estimated the annual deadweight cost of Christmas at $4 billion in 1992 terms, which translate to almost $8 billion in 2021 terms.

[11] See https://aflcio.org/executive-paywatch/highest-paid-ceos.

5.4   Why Do So Many People
Invest in Active Funds?

Passive investment has been steadily gaining popularity over the last decades. However, the amount of money invested in active funds is still about 6 times larger than the amount in passive funds. Figure 5.4 shows the aggregate size of U.S. active funds and passive funds over time. The top panel shows the aggregate dollar amounts. These have been growing roughly exponentially over time (note that the y-axis is logarithmic). The bottom panel shows the relative size of active and passive funds. In the 1990s, active funds managed about 40 times more money than passive funds. Passive funds gained popularity over time, and this ratio has been steadily decreasing, but it is still around 6 today. This means that for every dollar invested passively, there are $6 invested in active funds.

Some sophisticated investors may obtain abnormal returns by investing in active mutual funds (Gruber, 1996). For example, investors may employ the SAS described in the preceding chapter to identify the relatively few active funds that will outperform the market in the next period. However, the empirical evidence shows that the vast majority of investors would be better off by passively investing in the market. Active investors lose on average more than 2% per year, on a risk-adjusted basis, relative to passive investors. Despite this striking evidence, the active fund industry remains huge.

Why do so many investors invest in active funds? There are several possible explanations. Investors are human, and like most humans many of them suffer from a variety of systematic cognitive biases. Active mutual funds are highly motivated and efficient in exploiting these biases when marketing their products. For example, consider a mutual fund family managing several funds. In any given year, one of these funds is likely to achieve a return higher than the S&P 500 return. The mutual fund family will likely choose to advertise this particular fund, and not any of its underperforming sibling funds. Thus, investors observe a very biased sample of funds returns, which may lead to the wrong perception that most funds outperform the market, in stark contrast to the picture revealed by Figs. 5.2 and 5.3. In addition, funds have the freedom to choose the time-window for which they calculate their advertised return: a fund that had a high return in the last year, but a low return in the previous year, is likely to highlight last year's return in its advertisements. Most funds don't advertise long-run statistics or the standard deviation

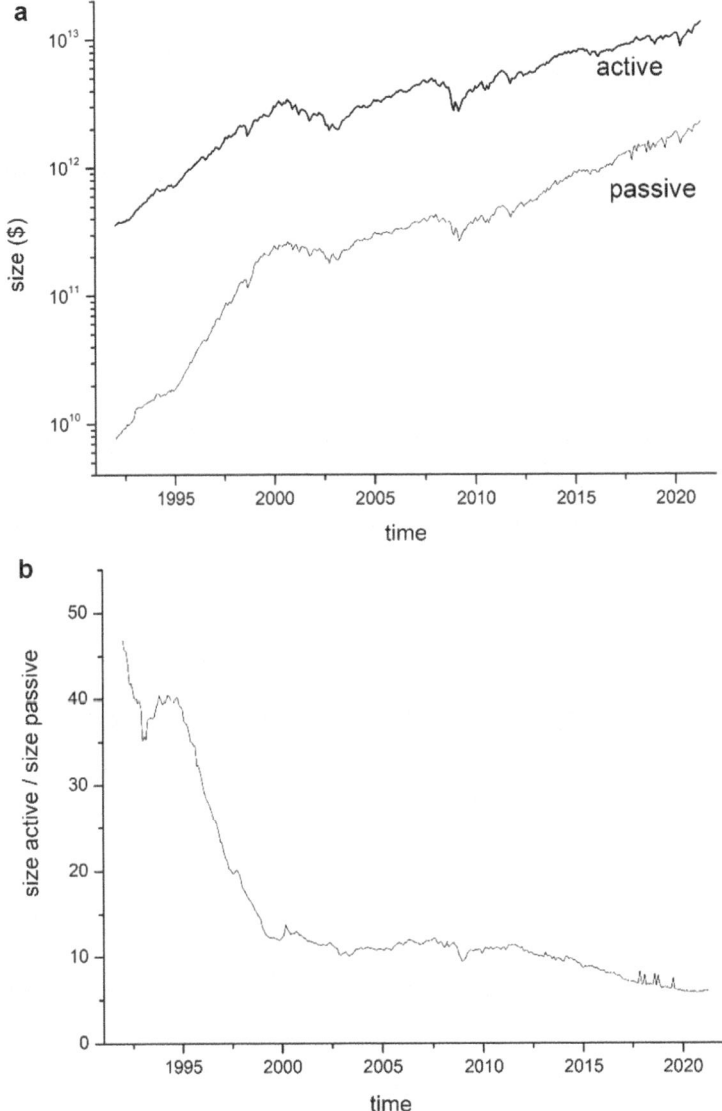

Fig. 5.4 The aggregate size of active and passive funds. Panel A shows the absolute dollar values. Panel B shows the ratio of active to passive funds. In the 1990s, active funds managed about 40 times more money than passive funds. This ratio has steadily decreased to about 6 today

of their returns at all (Jones & Smythe, 2003; Mullainathan & Shleifer, 2005). A more subtle strategy employed by some fund families is the incubation strategy: privately starting several new funds, and after a few years, shutting down those that did not do well and making public only those who did. This leads to a biased track record of the surviving funds, which Evans (2010) estimates as a 3.5% extra return over the incubation period. Evans shows that this outperformance attracts flows into these funds, but disappears in the post-incubation period.

Several well-known behavioral biases make investors very susceptible to the above practices. The belief in the "law of small numbers" (Rabin, 2002; Tversky & Kahneman, 1971) may make investors regard recent returns as much more representative of the return population than they actually are. The analysis in Chapter 4 reveals just how important this effect is: good out-of-sample performance is obtained only if one attaches a small weight to the in-sample return parameters, and a large weight to fees. The "hot hands" illusion (Gilovich et al., 1985; Rabin & Vayanos, 2010) makes investors imagine trends in the sequence of historical returns, even when such trends do not actually exist. The availability heuristic (Tversky & Kahneman, 1973) makes it hard to account for the selection bias in the observed sample. As information about the unsuccessful funds is not easily available, it is hard for investors to correct for the bias introduced by the advertisement of only those funds that have been successful (Wu, 2009), and by fund incubation. In addition, overconfidence and biased self-attribution (Bem, 1965; Daniel et al., 1998; De Bondt & Thaler, 1990; Oskamp, 1965) may make investors overestimate their fund selection ability.

The main alternative for active equity management is passive investing in the market index, e.g. the S&P500, either through index funds or index ETFs. These passive funds are typically advantageous in terms of performance, but are disadvantageous in terms of marketing ability. It is easier to market the small percentage of funds that happened to achieve higher returns than the market over a given time-frame, than it is to market the benchmark index itself. Index funds cannot boost performance via selection bias. And after all, "benchmark performance" sounds rather mundane, even though it turns out to be superior to the performance of most active funds.

5.5 SUMMARY

Active funds play an important role in the market. They gather and analyze information, and by doing so make market prices more efficient. Economic theory predicts that the fund managers most talented at collecting and analyzing information will become active managers, and will be compensated for their talent and effort by fees (Grossman & Stiglitz, 1980). The more there are active managers, the more efficient the market, and the smaller the rewards to being active. In equilibrium, we would expect the amount of active investments to be such that active and passive investments yield similar net risk-adjusted returns.

The empirical evidence is that the vast majority of active funds, about 92%, underperform relative to the passive market index. This suggest that the market is *not* in the above theoretical equilibrium—there is too much money invested actively. This inefficiency comes at a huge cost. The active mutual fund industry yields an annual loss of roughly $235 billion in the U.S. market, relative to passive indexing. This loss can be decomposed into an inefficient portfolio composition component of $186 billion, and a $49 billion component which is a wealth transfer from investors to funds as fees.

About 8% of active funds do beat the market on a risk-adjusted basis. Furthermore, as Chapter 4 shows, it may be possible to identify these funds ex-ante, via SAS or other sophisticated methods. However, investors who are considering active funds must be aware of two facts: (1) The unconditional odds are against them: 92% of active funds underperform, and many do so miserably—see Figs. 5.2 and 5.3. (2) Identifying the minority of funds that will outperform in the future is difficult—the relationship between past performance and future performance is very weak (see Figs. 4.1 and 4.2 in the preceding chapter). For those who are not discouraged by these two facts, the SAS presented in Chapter 4 may prove as a valuable tool for selecting active mutual funds.

REFERENCES

Axelson, U., & Bond, P. (2015). Wall street occupations. *The Journal of Finance, 70*(5), 1949–1996.

Bebchuk, L. A., & Fried, J. M. (2003). Executive compensation as an agency problem. *Journal of Economic Perspectives, 17*(3), 71–92.

Bebchuk, L. A., & Fried, J. M. (2009). *Pay without performance: The unfulfilled promise of executive compensation.* Harvard University Press.

Bem, D. J. (1965). An experimental analysis of self-persuasion. *Journal of Experimental Social Psychology, 1*(3), 199–218.

Berk, J. B., & Green, R. C. (2004). Mutual fund flows and performance in rational markets. *Journal of Political Economy, 112*(6), 1269–1295.

Berk, J. B., & van Binsbergen, J. H. (2015). Measuring skill in the mutual fund industry. *Journal of Financial Economics, 118*(1), 1–20.

Bertrand, M., & Mullainathan, S. (2001). Are CEOs rewarded for luck? The ones without principals are. *The Quarterly Journal of Economics, 116*(3), 901–932.

Browning, E. K. (1976). The marginal cost of public funds. *Journal of Political Economy, 84*(2), 283–298.

Carhart, M. M. (1997). On persistence in mutual fund performance. *The Journal of Finance, 52*(1), 57–82.

Cremers, K. M., & Grinstein, Y. (2014). Does the market for CEO talent explain controversial CEO pay practices? *Review of Finance, 18*(3), 921–960.

Daniel, K., Hirshleifer, D., & Subrahmanyam, A. (1998). Investor psychology and security market under-and overreactions. *Journal of Finance, 1998*, 1839–1885.

De Bondt, W. F., & Thaler, R. H. (1990). Do security analysts overreact? *The American Economic Review, 1990*, 52–57.

Evans, R. B. (2010). Mutual fund incubation. *The Journal of Finance, 65*(4), 1581–1611.

Fama, E. F., & French, K. R. (1995). Size and book-to-market factors in earnings and returns. *The Journal of Finance, 50*(1), 131–155.

Fama, E. F., & French, K. R. (2015). A five-factor asset pricing model. *Journal of Financial Economics, 116*(1), 1–22.

Gabaix, X., & Landier, A. (2008). Why has CEO pay increased so much? *The Quarterly Journal of Economics, 123*(1), 49–100.

Galton, F. (1907). Vox populi. *Nature, 75*, 450–451.

Gilovich, T., Vallone, R., & Tversky, A. (1985). The hot hand in basketball: On the misperception of random sequences. *Cognitive Psychology, 17*(3), 295–314.

Goergen, M., & Renneboog, L. (2011). Managerial compensation. *Journal of Corporate Finance, 17*(4), 1068–1077.

Grossman, S. J., & Stiglitz, J. E. (1980). On the impossibility of informationally efficient markets. *The American Economic Review, 70*(3), 393–408.

Gruber, M. J. (1996). Another puzzle: The growth in actively managed mutual funds. *The Journal of Finance, 51*(3), 783–810.

Hubbard, R. G. (2005). Pay without performance: A market equilibrium critique. *Journal of Corporation Law, 30*(4), 717.

Jones, M. A., & Smythe, T. (2003). The information content of mutual fund print advertising. *Journal of Consumer Affairs, 37*(1), 22–41.

Levhari, D., & Levy, H. (1977). The capital asset pricing model and the investment horizon. *The Review of Economics and Statistics, 1977*, 92–104.

Levy, H. (2016). *Stochastic dominance: Investment decision making under uncertainty.* Springer.

Levy, M. (2023). The deadweight loss of active management. *The Journal of Investing, 32*, 17–41.

Mullainathan, S., & Shleifer, A. (2005). *Persuasion in finance.* National Bureau of Economic Research (No. w11838).

Newman, H. A., & Mozes, H. A. (1999). Does the composition of the compensation committee influence CEO compensation practices? *Financial Management, 1999*, 41–53.

Oskamp, S. (1965). Overconfidence in case-study judgments. *Journal of Consulting Psychology, 29*(3), 261.

Oyer, P. (2004). Why do firms use incentives that have no incentive effects? *The Journal of Finance, 59*(4), 1619–1650.

Rabin, M. (2002). Inference by believers in the law of small numbers. *The Quarterly Journal of Economics, 117*(3), 775–816.

Rabin, M., & Vayanos, D. (2010). The gambler's and hot-hand fallacies: Theory and applications. *The Review of Economic Studies, 77*(2), 730–778.

Rappaport, A., & Nodine, T. (1999). New thinking on how to link executive pay with performance. *Harvard Business Review, 77*(2), 91–92.

Roll, R. (1994). What every CFO should know about scientific progress in financial economics: What is known and what remains to be resolved. *Financial Management, 23*(2), 69–75.

Surowiecki, J. (2005). *The wisdom of crowds.* Anchor.

Tervio, M. (2008). The difference that CEOs make: An assignment model approach. *American Economic Review, 98*(3), 642–668.

Tobin, J. (1965). The theory of portfolio selection. In F. H. Hahn and F. P. R Brechling (eds.) *The Theory of Interest Rates*, MacMillan, London.

Tversky, A., & Kahneman, D. (1971). Belief in the law of small numbers. *Psychological Bulletin, 76*(2), 105.

Tversky, A., & Kahneman, D. (1973). Availability: A heuristic for judging frequency and probability. *Cognitive Psychology, 5*(2), 207–232.

Waldfogel, J. (1993). The deadweight loss of Christmas. *The American Economic Review, 83*(5), 1328–1336.

Wu, C. (2009). Mutual fund advertisements. *Investment Management and Financial Innovations, 6*, 68–76.

CHAPTER 6

Target Date Funds, and How to Improve Them

Abstract Human capital is an important component of the investor's total portfolio, of which the financial portfolio constitutes only one part. The value of human capital, which is typically considered "bond like", generally declines after middle age. Thus, in order to keep the asset allocation in the total portfolio constant over time, investors should decrease the allocation to equities in their financial portfolios. Target date funds offer a convenient way to do so: they follow a predetermined linear "glide path" of reducing the allocation to equities. However, linear glide paths are sub-optimal. Switching from linear to exponential glide paths typically improves investors' welfare by 10–30%.

Keywords Target date funds · Lifecycle funds · Glide path · Exponential glide path

One of the central goals of investing is saving for retirement. Many academics and practitioners recommend starting the life cycle with a high allocation to equities, and gradually shifting to safer bonds as one ages. This is captured by the famous rule of thumb stating that the percentage an investor should allocate to stocks is 100 minus the investor's age. According to this rule, a 30-year-old should allocate 70% to stocks and 30% to bonds, while a 60-year-old should allocate only 40% to stocks. A

M. Levy and R. Roll, *Mutual Fund Selection*,
https://doi.org/10.1007/978-3-031-69758-6_6

young person can afford the exposure to higher-risk-higher-reward stocks because there are more years to recover from a stock market downturn, for example, by working longer and postponing retirement. An older person does not have the same flexibility.

Paradoxically, the rule of thumb above actually reduces the variation in the asset allocation over time, rather than increases it (more on this in the next section). Importantly, this recognizes that an investor's *total* portfolio includes both *financial* savings and human capital, (which is the present value of future labor income). For a young person, the human capital component constitutes a large part of the total portfolio. This component is supposedly rather safe, and is typically considered "bond like". Thus, to keep asset allocation in the total portfolio constant, a young investor should invest a large proportion of her financial portfolio in stocks. As the investor ages, the human capital component decreases, and the size of financial portfolio on average increases. Thus, to maintain a constant allocation, the investor should gradually shift from stocks to bonds.

Target date funds, which are also known as lifecycle funds, offer investors an easy way to decrease the allocation to equities over time: the fund does it for them. If you expect to retire in 2070, for example, you can invest in a fund with a target date of 2070. The fund reduces the allocation to stocks over time, down to a lower limit on the target date. The pattern of the reduction is called the fund's "glide path". A typical glide path of a target date fund with a target date of year 2070 is shown in Fig. 6.1. Target date funds differ in their target dates, the point at which the allocation to equities starts to decline, and the steepness of the glide path, but almost all funds employ a *linear* glide path (Ibbotson, 2008).

Target date funds offer investors an important service, and have therefore become very popular. According to the ICI 2023 yearbook, as of the end of 2022, target date funds manage over $1.5 trillion in the U.S., and 59% of investors in 401(k) plans invest at least part of their money in these funds.

While target date funds help reduce time variation in the asset allocation of the total portfolio, they typically introduce two systematic biases. Both of these biases are easy to correct, and these corrections lead to a substantial improvement in investors' welfare. To analyze this situation and explain the problem, we begin by discussing the benefits of keeping the asset allocation (in the total portfolio) constant. Section 6.2 describes the systematic biases of existing target date funds. Section 6.3

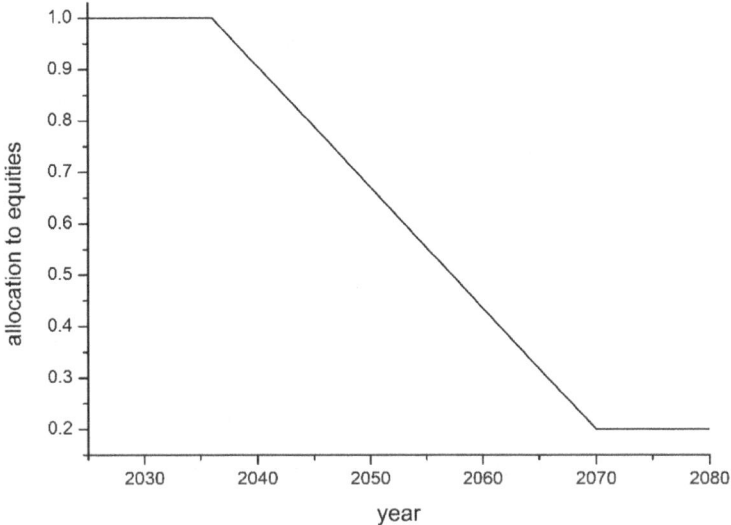

Fig. 6.1 A typical allocation to equities in a target date fund with the target date of 2070. Almost all funds employ a linear "glide path" to determine the reduction to equities over time

offers a simple way to alleviate these biases. The improvement in investors' welfare due to the correction is analyzed in Sect. 6.4. We conclude with a summary of the key take-away message in Sect. 6.5.

6.1 THE ADVANTAGES OF CONSTANT ASSET ALLOCATION

To get an intuition about the benefits of maintaining a constant asset allocation in the total portfolio, consider the following simple example, inspired by Samuelson (1989). There are two investors: Investor A maintains a constant allocation of 50% in stocks and 50% in bonds. Investor B spends half of the time fully invested in stocks, and the other half fully invested bonds. Thus, both investors have the same average allocation of 50% in stocks. Assume, for simplicity, that in every period, stocks yield a rate of return of either 30% or − 10% with equal probabilities, while bonds yield a sure return of 3%. Suppose that the investors invest for 4 periods, and consider the "typical" case where stocks go up in two periods and go down in the other two. In this case, the total return of investor A is:

$$R_A = \left(\frac{1}{2}(0.9 + 1.03)\right)^2 \left(\frac{1}{2}(1.3 + 1.03)\right)^2 = 1.264. \qquad (6.1)$$

If investor B does not have the ability to time the market,[1] and invests in stocks during one "up" and one "down" period, his total return is:

$$R_B = 0.9 \cdot 1.3 \cdot 1.03^2 = 1.241. \qquad (6.2)$$

In this "typical" case, investor A, who maintains a constant allocation, ends up better off than investor B, who changes allocations over time. This hints that a constant asset allocation may be advantageous to changing it over time. But, of course, this is just one possible case. If investor B happens to bet on the stock in the two "up" periods, he will obviously do better than investor A. Conversely, if he unluckily bets on the stock in the two "down" periods, he will do much worse than investor A. For 4 investment periods and a stock that has only two possible returns, we have 16 scenarios for the stock returns, and the total return of investor B depends on how lucky his timing guesses are. In some scenarios, investor A is better off, and in others, investor B does better.

In general, if one investor determines his asset allocation in each period by a random draw from some distribution, while the other maintains the same average allocation but holds it constant over time, the distribution of returns implied by a constant allocation dominates the random allocation strategy. This result is well known for all Constant Relative Risk Averse (CRRA) investors (Hakansson, 1970; Leland, 1969; Merton, 1969; Merton & Samuelson, 1974; Samuelson, 1969), and was recently generalized to all risk averters (Levy & Levy, 2021). Technically speaking, Levy and Levy (2021) prove that $\tilde{R}_A$ dominates $\tilde{R}_B$ by SSD, where $\tilde{R}_B$ is the terminal return distribution to any strategy with stochastic allocation, and $\tilde{R}_A$ is the return distribution to the constant allocation strategy with the same average allocation. This is true for any distribution of stock returns, and any distribution of random asset allocation.

---

[1] If the market is perfectly efficient, no investors are able to time the market. However, the empirical evidence suggests that markets may not always be efficient (Lo 2017; Lo and MacKinlay 2011).

If the asset allocation of the investor who changes it over time is not drawn randomly, but is instead predetermined, the dominance of constant allocation does not necessarily hold. For example, if there are T investment periods, and investor B decides to invest in the stock for the first $T/2$ periods and to invest in the bond in the remaining periods, some risk averters may prefer the distribution of $\tilde{R}_B$ over the distribution of $\tilde{R}_A$, where $\tilde{R}_A$ is the return to holding a constant allocation of 50% in the stock (Table 1 in Levy & Levy, 2021 provides such an example). However, as the number of investment periods increases, the SSD dominance of $\tilde{R}_A$ over $\tilde{R}_B$ emerges, even in the case of a predetermined allocation that changes over time (see Levy & Levy, 2021, Sect. 3.2.1).

Changing the asset allocation over time affects both the expected return and the variance of returns. Consider any strategy of changing the asset allocation over time in a predetermined way, such as a strategy of investing 80% in the stock in the first 5 periods, and 50% in the rest of the periods, or a strategy of investing 60% in the stock in even years, and 30% in odd years. Levy (2023) shows that for any such strategy, a constant allocation strategy with the same average allocation yields a higher expected return. The magnitude of this effect, however, is small. The main difference between constant and time-varying allocation is due to the volatility.

The following example provides an idea about the magnitude of the above effects. Consider two investors who invest for 120 months. There are two assets: a risk-free bond yielding a sure monthly return of 0.3%, and a stock index with monthly returns drawn randomly and independently from a normal distribution with a mean of 1% and a standard deviation of 5% (these values are pretty close to the empirical values of T-bills and the S&P 500 index). Investor A maintains a constant allocation of 50% in each of the two assets. Investor B invests in the stock for 60 months, and in the bond in the remaining 60 months (as the returns are i.i.d., it doesn't matter how the investor chooses these 60 months). The top panel of Fig. 6.2 shows the distribution of 120-month returns for these two strategies, i.e. the distributions of terminal wealth after 120 months for an initial investment of $1. These distributions are calculated numerically. The constant allocation strategy yields a slightly higher expected return: 93.1% compared to 92.7% for the time-varying allocation strategy. The difference in the standard deviations is much more dramatic: 53.6% for the constant allocation strategy versus 76.5% for the time-varying allocation strategy. The intuition for this difference is straightforward:

time varying allocation leads to more extreme results—if the 60 months invested in the stock happen to be on average high-return months, the result of the time-varying strategy is spectacular; if they happen to be low-return months, the result can be catastrophic.

Had the distributions of total return after 120 months been normal, the fact that the constant allocation strategy yields a higher mean and a lower standard deviation would have sufficed to determine its dominance for all risk averters. But as the figure shows, the distributions are positively skewed, hence they are obviously not normal. In the case of non-normal distributions, we can employ the stochastic dominance criterion to determine whether dominance exists. The bottom panel of the figure shows the two cumulative distribution functions. The figure reveals that the constant

Fig. 6.2 The distributions of total return after 120 months. Panel A shows the probability density functions, and panel B shows the cumulative distribution functions. The bold lines depict the case of a constant allocation of 50% to the stock and 50% to the risk-free bond, while the thin lines depict the case of investing in the stock 50% of the time (60 months), and investing in the bond in the remaining periods. The "+" area in Panel B is greater than the "-" area, indicating that the constant allocation strategy dominates the time-varying allocation strategy by SSD

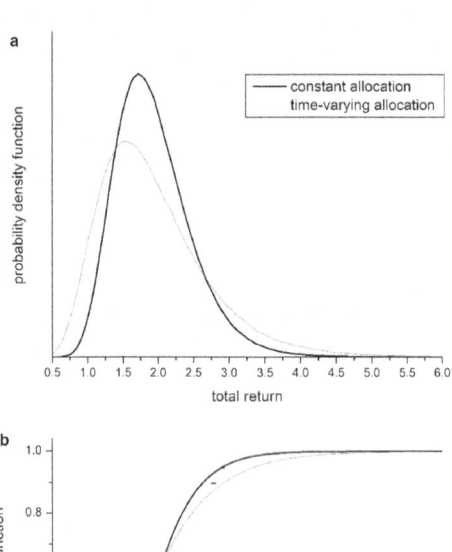

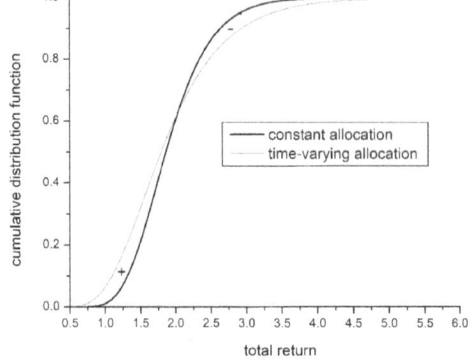

allocation strategy dominates the time-varying strategy by SSD: the "+" area where the constant allocation CDF is below the time-varying CDF is larger than the "-" area, where the opposite holds.[2] This is consistent with the general result of Levy and Levy (2021) about the emergence of SSD as the number of periods becomes large. Levy (2023) provides a formula for the risk-adjusted excess return of constant allocation versus switching from the stock to the bond, and estimates this excess return as about 1.3% on an annual basis.

To summarize, risk averters are generally better off maintaining a constant asset allocation rather than changing it over time. The difference is economically significant, primarily due to the lower volatility implied by constant allocation. Thus, investors should aim to hold their asset allocation constant over time. Crucially, this holds for the asset allocation in their *total portfolio*, which includes not only their financial portfolio, but their human capital as well. Target date funds help in approaching this goal, by reducing the allocation to equity as the investor ages, and her human capital diminishes. However, as the next section shows, target date funds suffer from two systematic biases, both of which can be easily remedied.

6.2 The Systematic Biases of Target Date Funds

Target date funds help in reducing the variation in the asset allocation of the investor's total portfolio. These funds manage the investor's financial portfolio (or at least part of it), and they gradually reduce the allocation to (riskier) equities over time. This mitigates the concurrent reduction in the investor's human capital. Conversely, if the fund had maintained a constant asset allocation, then as human capital diminished with age, the total allocation to stocks would have increased. Thus, reducing the allocation to equities in the financial portfolio over time makes sense. While providing a valuable service, target date funds suffer from two systematic biases. These biases are due to the predetermined linear glide path, employed by virtually all target date funds. In this section, we describe these biases, and in the next section, we describe a simple way to fix them.

The two biases are:

---

[2] This implies dominance by SSD: see Eq. 3.4 in Chapter 3 for the SSD criterion. Levy (2016) provides more detail, and the graphical interpretation of SSD.

(B1) **No Adjustments to Market Fluctuations**

The investor's financial portfolio is only a part of his total portfolio, the other part being his human capital. Market fluctuations change the relative weights of these two components, and require the fund to make adjustments in order to keep the asset allocation in the total allocation constant. Target date funds typically don't make such adjustments. As a result, market fluctuations are translated to fluctuations in the investors' asset allocation. The following example may illustrate. Consider an investor who has $100 of financial wealth invested in a target date fund, and $100 of human capital (HC). Suppose that the fund invests 80% in equities. Thus, the proportions in the investor's total portfolio are 40% in stocks and 60% in bonds: the investor holds $80 in stocks and $120 in bonds ($20 in the fund + $100 HC). Consider what happens when the stock market goes up by 20% and the bond value does not change. The increase in the stock price now makes the financial portfolio worth $116 (as the value of stocks increases to $96), and the value of the investor's total portfolio increases to $216. If the fund maintains its policy of 80% investment in equities, this implies that the allocation to equities in the investor's total portfolio goes up from 40% to about 43%: (80% × 116/216 = 43%). This is because the weight of the financial portfolio in the total portfolio has increased. If the asset allocation in the investor's total portfolio is to be kept at 40%, the fund must reduce its allocation in equities to 74.5%: 74.5% × 116/216 = 40%. Similarly, when the stock market goes down, the fund should increase its allocation to equities in order to keep the allocation in the total portfolio constant.

(B2) **Linearity of the Glide Path**

Almost all target date funds reduce the allocation to equities linearly. The linear glide path, as shown for example in Figure 6.1, is simple, and it resonates with the popular rule-of-thumb of allocating a percentage of 100-age to equities. We will show below that the average weight of the human capital in the total portfolio decreases as an *exponential*, rather than a linear, function of time. This mismatch causes a systematic variation of the asset allocation in the total portfolio, as discussed below.

To formalize the above ideas, let's denote the investor's financial wealth by F, and his human capital wealth by HC. The investor's total wealth is $TW = F + HC$. Assume that human capital is bond like (or alternatively, that HC represents the bond-like component of human capital). Thus, the allocation to equities in the investor's total portfolio is given by:

$$w_{TOT} = \frac{w_F \cdot F}{TW} = \frac{w_F \cdot F}{F + HC}, \tag{6.3}$$

where w_{TOT} denotes the allocation to equities in the *total* portfolio, and w_F denotes the allocation to equities in the *financial* portfolio, i.e. in the target date fund. We can thus express w_F as a function of w_{TOT}:

$$w_F = \frac{w_{TOT} \cdot TW}{F} = w_{TOT}\left(1 + \frac{HC}{F}\right). \tag{6.4}$$

If one wishes to keep w_{TOT} at a constant level, c, w_F should change with F and HC according to:

$$w_F = c \cdot \frac{TW}{F} = c \cdot \left(1 + \frac{HC}{F}\right). \tag{6.5}$$

This expression demonstrates the two systematic biases mentioned above. (B1): the investor's financial wealth F fluctuates with the market; therefore, the allocation to equities in the financial portfolio, w_F, should also respond to market fluctuations—when the market goes up, w_F should be reduced, and vice versa. (B2): the ratio $\frac{HC}{F}$ decreases over time, but not linearly: financial wealth increases *on average* exponentially. Therefore, a linear glide path implies a systematic variation in w_{TOT}, rather than the desired goal of keeping it constant.

Figure 6.3 provides a perspective about the magnitude of these biases. It describes the portfolio holdings of an investor entering the market at the age of 20, until he reaches the age of 90. Initially, the investor's human capital is assumed to be equal to his financial wealth, i.e. $\frac{HC_0}{F_0} = 1$ (which implies $\frac{HC_0}{TW_0} = 0.5$, recall that $F + HC = TW$). The investor invests his financial wealth in a target date fund with the typical glide path shown in the top panel. This represents the investor's allocation to equities in his financial portfolio, i.e. w_F. At any given point in time, we define the investor's human capital as the present value of all his future savings, i.e. labor income minus consumption.[3] To simplify the analysis, we make the assumption that saving is constant over time. This implies that the value of HC is an annuity with a terminal date at age 90. Stock returns are drawn randomly (with replacement) from the historical annual U.S. market returns (1927–2018 sample). The average T-bill rate over the same period, 3.4%, serves as the risk-free rate. We simulate 100,000 "life histories", i.e. 100,000 realizations of stock returns during the investor's 70-year financial horizon. For each such history, we record the evolution of the investor's financial portfolio, his total portfolio, and w_{TOT}, the allocation to equities in his total portfolio.

The thin lines in Panel B of Fig. 6.3 depict w_{TOT} for five different "histories". They differ one from the other due to the different realizations of stock returns in each history. The bold line shows the average w_{TOT} across all 100,000 simulated histories. This figure illustrates the two biases of target dates following linear glide paths. The linear reduction to equities in the target date funds is misaligned with the average exponential increase in value of the financial portfolio (bias B2). This implies that the allocation to equities in the total portfolio is too high in the early years, peaks at ages 40–50, and drops too low in later years, as shown by the bold line in Panel B. The effect is large—rather than obtaining the desired goal of a constant w_{TOT}, the allocation changes over the life-cycle from a high of almost 90% to a low of 20%. Market fluctuations add noise on top of this systematic bias. The fact that the fund does not adjust its asset allocation to market fluctuations (bias B1) leads to an additional "noise" element in w_{TOT}, as evident in the different paths of w_{TOT} across different histories (the thin lines). Both of these biases can be corrected quite easily, as discussed in the next section.

6.3   A Simple Fix

The systematic bias (B2), which causes the "hump" of the average asset allocation, w_{TOT}, can be overcome by adopting a non-linear glide path. This glide path should be the solution of (6.5) for the average path of the financial wealth F. Note that both the financial wealth, F, and the

---

[3] This definition is not standard, as human capital typically refers to the present value of labor income, and is separated from consumption. In our context, the relevant value is income minus consumption, i.e. savings. For example, if consumption is equal to income, i.e. there are no savings, the individual's financial portfolio is his total portfolio.

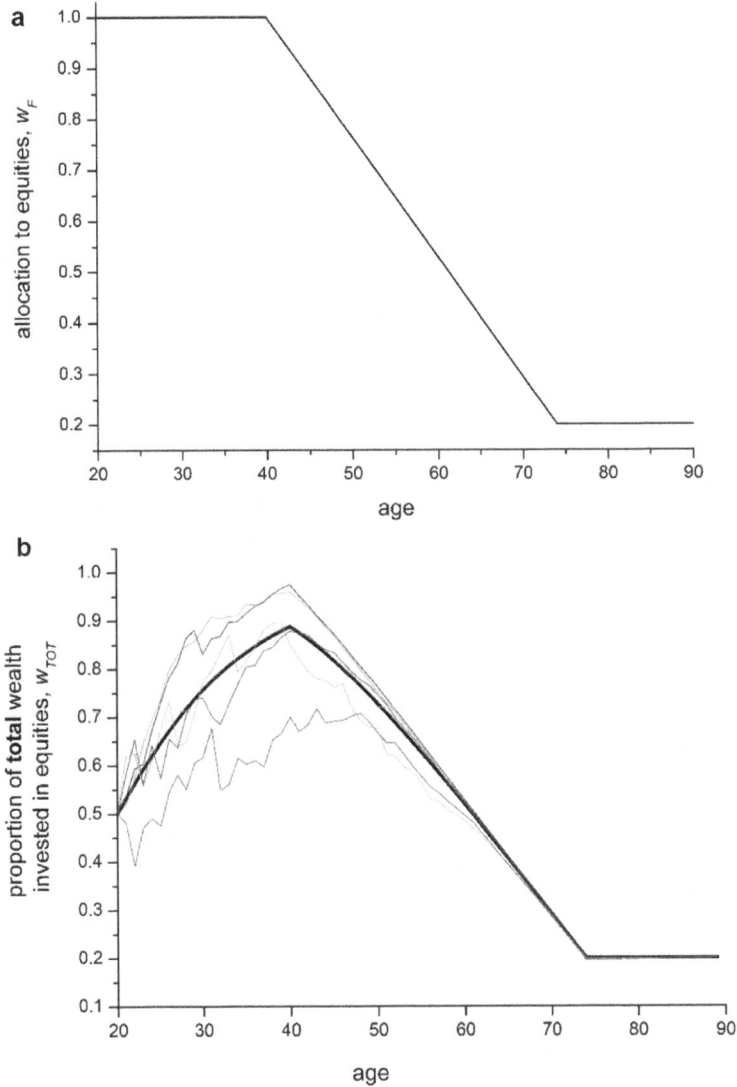

Fig. 6.3 Panel B shows the allocation to equities in the total portfolio, w_{TOT}, for an investor investing in a target date fund with the linear glide path shown in Panel A. The thin lines represent w_{TOT} in 5 different "histories", each one with a different realization of the stochastic market returns. The bold line shows the average w_{TOT} across 100,000 simulated histories. The "hump" of the bold line is due to bias (B2), while the variations from one history to another are due to the lack of adjustments to market fluctuations (bias B1)

human capital, HC, are time-dependent, and therefore, so is w_F. The difficulty of solving this equation stems from the fact that the financial wealth at time t is a function of the asset allocation in the financial portfolio, w_F, throughout all time periods leading up to time t. Thus, F in the denominator of (6.5) is itself an integral function of $w_F(t)$. Levy and Levy (2021) show that this non-linear differential equation can be solved by the Riccati method, leading to the following solution:

$$w_F(t) = \frac{c}{1 - e^{-c(r_m - r_f)t}\left(\frac{HC_0}{TW_0}\right)\left(\frac{e^{r_f(T-t)}-1}{e^{r_f T}-1}\right)}, \tag{6.6}$$

where r_f is the continuous risk-free return, r_m is the continuous expected return on equities, $\left(\frac{HC_0}{TW_0}\right)$ is the initial proportion of human capital in the total portfolio, T is the terminal date, and c is the desired constant allocation to equities in the total portfolio. This solution shows that the glide path that maintains a constant asset allocation in the total portfolio is exponential, rather than linear. Levy and Levy (2021) call this solution the "exponential glide path". While Eq. (6.6) is derived in the continuous-time setting, we will see below that it serves as an excellent approximation for the discrete-time solution. The exponential glide path describes the *average* optimal asset allocation, averaged across different realizations of the stock return process. Stated differently, if one ignores adjustments to stochastic market fluctuations, this is the glide path that should be followed. This glide path corrects the systematic bias (B2), but not bias (B1). It turns out that most of the improvement in the investor's welfare comes from this correction to the average allocation, as will be shown in the next section.

The bold line in the top panel of Fig. 6.4 depicts the exponential glide path given by Eq. (6.6) for the same parameters employed in the simulations of the previous section: the investor's financial horizon is 90 years ($T = 90$), and his initial human capital is half of his initial total wealth $\frac{HC_0}{TW_0} = 0.5$. The return parameters are taken as $r_f = 0.033$, and $r_m = 0.095$, which are the continuously compounded values of the empirical average returns employed in the previous section. The level of the allocation to the stock in the total portfolio, c, determines the aggressiveness of the fund. In order to estimate the welfare improvement implied by the exponential glide path relative to the linear glide path, we set c to the same value as the average allocation in the total portfolio when following the linear glide path, which is 53.6% (this is the average value of w_{TOT} in the simulations shown in Fig. 6.3).

Following the exponential glide path does not eliminate all variation in w_{TOT}, unless adjustments to market fluctuations are made. This is shown by the thin lines in the bottom panel of Fig. 6.4, which show w_{TOT} for 5 different "life histories" (i.e. 5 realizations of the return process). The bold line shows w_{TOT} averaged over all 100,000 histories. The figure shows that the exponential glide path eliminates the systematic deviation from constant allocation: compare the bold lines in the bottom panels of Figs. 6.3 and 6.4. Thus, the exponential glide path corrects bias (B2). In order to correct bias (B1) as well, one should adjust the allocation in the financial portfolio to market fluctuations. The 5 thin lines in the top panel of Fig. 6.4 show the values of w_F needed to keep w_{TOT} constant at the value $c = 0.536$. The dashed line shows the average w_F across the 100,000 simulated histories. This dashed line is almost indistinguishable from the theoretical exponential glide path (the bold line). This again indicates that the exponential glide path eliminates the systematic bias (B2). It also indicates that the continuous-time solution in Eq. (6.6) serves as an excellent approximation for the discrete-time setting employed in the simulation.

6.4   The Welfare Benefits of Exponential Glide Paths

To estimate the welfare gain obtained by switching from a linear glide path to an exponential glide path, we calculate the certainty equivalents of the terminal wealth distributions (over all 100,000 simulated histories) under the two settings. The welfare gain is measured by the relative increase in the certainty equivalent:

$$\Delta CE \equiv \frac{CE_{\text{exponential}}}{CE_{\text{linear}}} - 1. \tag{6.7}$$

We calculate this gain for different utility functions and different values of the initial weight of human capital in the total portfolio, $\frac{HC_0}{TW_0}$. We examine the two most commonly employed preference classes: Constant Relative Risk Aversion (CRRA) of the form $U(W) = \frac{1}{1-\gamma} W^{1-\gamma}$, where W denotes wealth and γ is the relative risk aversion coefficient, and negative exponential preferences: $U(W) = -e^{-bW}$. Tables 6.1 and 6.2 report the

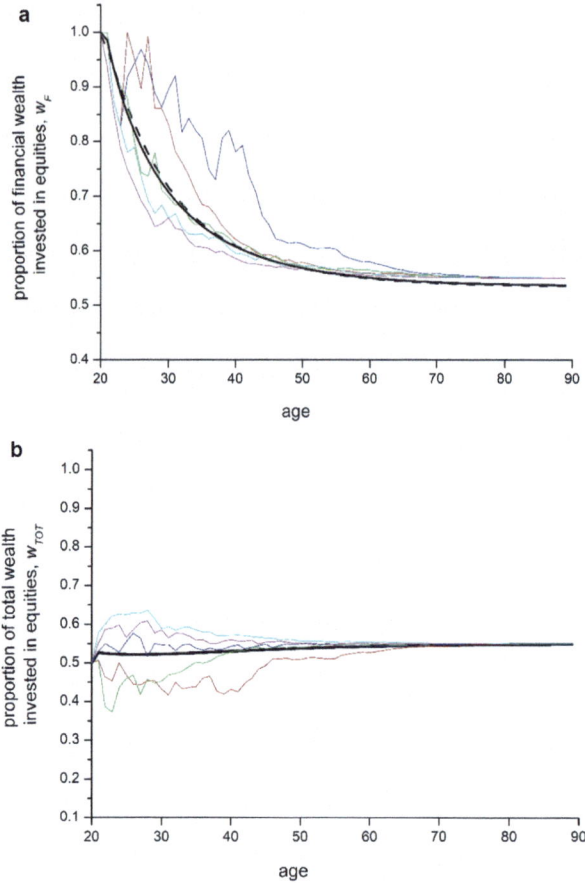

Fig. 6.4 The Exponential Glide Path. The bold line in the top panel shows the exponential glide path, given by Eq. (6.6), for the same parameters employed in the previous section (Fig. 6.3). The top panel shows the allocation to equities in the financial portfolio. The thin lines represent the w_F needed to keep w_{TOT} exactly constant, in 5 different "histories", each one with a different realization of the stochastic market returns. The dashed line shows the average value of these w_Fs across 100,000 simulated histories. The dashed line almost perfectly coincides with the theoretical exponential glide path, indicating that the exponential glide path eliminates the systematic bias (B2). The bottom panel shows w_{TOT} in the same 5 histories, if the target date fund follows the exponential glide path, but does not adjust its allocation to market fluctuations. The bold line shows the average value across all 100,000 simulations

values of ΔCE obtained. Table 6.1 shows the gain when the asset allocation in the total portfolio is kept exactly constant, i.e. both biases (B1) and (B2) are corrected. Table 6.2 shows the gain when the fund employs the exponential glide path, but does not adjust its allocation in response to market fluctuations, i.e. only bias (B2) is corrected. As in the previous section, the average total allocation is the same under all settings ($c = 0.536$), thus, the level of the allocation is the same, and the entire welfare gain is due to the reduction in the variation of w_{TOT} over time.

When the fund follows the exponential glide path and it also adjusts to market fluctuations, i.e. w_{TOT} is kept exactly constant, the gain is higher than when the exponential glide path is followed, but no adjustments to market fluctuations are made: the number in every cell of Table 6.1 is larger than the corresponding number in Table 6.2. However, the extra gain by adjusting to market fluctuations is small. Almost all of the gain is obtained by employing the exponential glide path instead of the linear glide path. Thus, from a practical perspective, if target date funds simply replace their linear glide paths with exponentially decreasing glide paths, they will obtain almost the same certainty equivalent gain for their investors, as if they kept w_{TOT} exactly constant by also adjusting the allocations to market fluctuations.

Table 6.1 The welfare gain, ΔCE, in %, when the asset allocation in the total portfolio is kept exactly constant

CRRA preferences, γ	Initial weight of human capital in total portfolio, $\frac{HC_0}{TW_0}$								
	0.1	0.2	0.3	0.4	0.5	0.6	0.7	0.8	0.9
0.5	24.0	22.2	20.6	19.1	16.9	14.0	10.5	6.5	1.9
1	34.4	30.9	28.1	25.5	22.6	19.1	15.3	11.0	6.4
2	64.3	49.8	42.0	36.6	31.9	27.3	22.9	18.6	13.9
3	118.7	71.6	52.6	42.5	35.7	30.4	26.2	22.3	18.4
4	165.4	90.9	59.6	43.8	34.4	28.1	24.1	21.0	18.2
Negative exponential preferences, b									
1	13.4	13.0	12.6	12.3	11.6	10.5	9.3	8.4	8.5
10	20.3	19.3	18.2	17.2	16.0	14.8	13.7	13.3	14.8

Table 6.2 The welfare gain, ΔCE, in %, when the exponential glide path is followed, but no adjustments to market fluctuations are made

CRRA preferences, γ	Initial weight of human capital in total portfolio, $\frac{HC_0}{TW_0}$								
	0.1	0.2	0.3	0.4	0.5	0.6	0.7	0.8	0.9
0.5	23.4	21.1	19.0	17.1	15.0	12.3	9.0	5.1	0.6
1	33.8	29.9	26.6	23.8	21.0	17.7	14.1	10.0	5.4
2	62.4	47.7	39.8	34.2	29.7	25.7	21.7	17.6	13.1
3	113.6	67.5	49.0	39.1	32.9	28.3	24.4	20.6	16.8
4	158.3	86.5	56.4	41.1	32.4	26.8	22.5	18.7	15.4
Negative exponential preferences, b									
1	13.2	12.5	12.0	11.5	10.9	10.0	9.1	8.4	8.3
10	20.0	18.6	17.2	15.8	14.3	12.7	11.2	10.0	9.7

The welfare gain depends on the individual's preferences as well as on the ratio $\frac{HC_0}{TW_0}$. CRRA preferences are generally considered to be much more realistic than the negative exponential CARA preferences (see, for example, Blume & Friend, 1975; Markowitz et al., 1994). Empirical and experimental estimates of the relative risk aversion coefficient, γ, are typically in the range 1–2 (Arrow, 1971; Dolde & Tobin, 1971; Kydland & Prescott, 1982; Hansen & Singleton, 1982; Szpiro, 1986a, 1986b, De Mel et al., 2008; Barro & Jin, 2011; Levy, 2024). Clearly, there is a great deal of heterogeneity across investors in the ratio $\frac{HC_0}{TW_0}$: while some may start their adult lives with almost no financial wealth, i.e. with $\frac{HC_0}{TW_0}$ close to 1, others inherit (or are expected to inherit) large financial wealth, and have $\frac{HC_0}{TW_0}$ close to 0. Levy and Levy (2021) suggest that $\frac{HC_0}{TW_0}$ values are typically in the range 0.5–0.8. These typical parameter values are highlighted in Tables 6.1 and 6.2. For these values, the welfare increase obtained by switching from a linear glide path to the exponentially decreasing glide path is in the order of 10–30%.

6.5   SUMMARY

Investors are generally better off keeping their asset allocation constant, rather than varying it over time. When considering their allocation, they should consider not only their financial portfolio (equities and possibly other risky assets, such as real estate), but also their total portfolio including human capital. Human capital is typically more "bond like" than "stock like", and it diminishes over time. Thus, in order to keep a constant allocation in the total portfolio, investors should gradually reduce their allocation to riskier assets in their financial portfolios over time.

Target date funds are very helpful in this respect. They offer investors an "automatic pilot" reduction in the allocation to equities. However, the linear glide path that they employ introduces a systematic bias in the asset allocation in the total portfolio: the allocation to equities is too high in the early years, peaks at middle age, and is too low at later years (see Fig. 6.3). An additional source of variation in the asset allocation is due to market fluctuations.

Levy and Levy (2021) show that in order to keep the asset allocation in the total portfolio constant over time, the glide path should be exponential, rather than linear. Switching from a linear glide path to an exponential one, while keeping the same average asset allocation, improves investors' welfare by 10–30% for typical parameter values. Adjusting to market fluctuations leads to a further improvement, but it is rather marginal relative to the effect of adopting an exponential glide path. To the best of our knowledge, as of 2024, no target date offers an exponential glide path. But the advantages are large, and in the future, this may well become the industry standard.

REFERENCES

Arrow, K. J. (1971). *Essays in the theory of risk-bearing*. North-Holland Pub. Co.

Barro, R. J., & Jin, T. (2011). On the size distribution of macroeconomic disasters. *Econometrica, 79*(5), 1567–1589.

Blume, M. E., & Friend, I. (1975). The asset structure of individual portfolios and some implications for utility functions. *The Journal of Finance, 30*(2), 585–603.

De Mel, S., McKenzie, D., & Woodruff, C. (2008). Returns to capital in microenterprises: Evidence from a field experiment. *The Quarterly Journal of Economics, 123*(4), 1329–1372.

Dolde, W., & Tobin, J. (1971). *Wealth, liquidity, and consumption (No. 311)*. Cowles Foundation for Research in Economics, Yale University.

Hakansson, N. H. (1970). Optimal investment and consumption strategies under risk for a class of utility functions. *Econometrica, 38*, 587–607.

Hansen, L. P., & Singleton, K. J. (1982). Generalized instrumental variables estimation of nonlinear rational expectations models. *Econometrica, 50*(5), 1269–1286.

Ibbotson Associates Research Paper—Lifetime Asset Allocations: Methodologies for Target Maturity Funds, 2008. https://corporate.morningstar.com/ib/documents/MethodologyDocuments/IBBAssociates/LifetimeAssetAllocMeth021108.pdf

Investment Company Institute (ICI). (2023). Factbook: https://www.ici.org/system/files/2023-05/2023-factbook.pdf

Kydland, F. E., & Prescott, E. C. (1982). Time to build and aggregate fluctuations. *Econometrica: Journal of the Econometric Society*, 1345–1370.

Leland, H. E. (1969). Dynamic portfolio theory. *The Journal of Finance, 24*(3), 543–544.

Levy, H. (2016). *Stochastic dominance: Investment decision making under uncertainty*. Springer.

Levy, H., & Levy, M. (2021). The cost of diversification over time, and a simple way to improve target-date funds. *Journal of Banking and Finance, 122*, 105995.

Levy, M. (2023). The cost of investment hubris. *Journal of Portfolio Management, 50*(1), 1–16.

Levy, M. (2024). Relative risk aversion must be close to 1. *Annals of Operations Research, 2024*, 1.

Lo, A. W. (2017). *Adaptive markets: Financial evolution at the speed of thought*. Princeton University Press.

Lo, A. W., & MacKinlay, A. C. (2011). *A non-random walk down Wall Street*. Princeton University Press.

Markowitz, H. M., Reid, D. W., & Tew, B. V. (1994). The value of a blank check. *Journal of Portfolio Management, 20*(4), 82.

Merton, R. C. (1969). Lifetime portfolio selection under uncertainty: The continuous-time case. *The Review of Economics and Statistics, 1969*, 247–257.

Merton, R. C., & Samuelson, P. A. (1974). Fallacy of the log-normal approximation to optimal portfolio decision-making over many periods. *Journal of Financial Economics, 1*(1), 67–94.

Samuelson, P. A. (1969). Lifetime portfolio selection by dynamic stochastic programming. *The Review of Economics and Statistics, 51*(3), 239–246.

Samuelson, P. A. (1989). The judgement of economic science on rational portfolio man. *Journal of Portfolio Management, 16*(1), 4.

Szpiro, G. G. (1986a). Measuring risk aversion: An alternative approach. *The Review of Economics and Statistics, 1986*, 156–159.

Szpiro, G. G. (1986b). Relative risk aversion around the world. *Economics Letters, 20*(1), 19–21.

CHAPTER 7

The Role of Luck

Abstract Luck plays a central and unavoidable role in determining investment and management success. This chapter quantifies the role of luck. Being aware of the importance of luck may help investors and managers avoid the pitfalls of overconfidence, and the substantial costs associated with them.

Keywords Luck · Randomness · Investment talent · CEO compensation · The distribution of wealth · Overconfidence

Success is most likely due to some combination of talent, effort, and luck. It is undisputable that talent and effort are important, but people have very different views about the relative importance of luck. Our beliefs about the importance of luck may affect our opinions about a variety of central economic issues, including inequality, taxation, and CEO compensation. Quantifying the role of luck also tells us what we can, or can't, expect as the benefits of informed mutual fund selection. We begin by providing an overall perspective about the role of luck in managerial success and investments, and then turn to discuss the implications for mutual fund selection.

7.1   LUCK AND CEO PERFORMANCE

Successful CEOs are highly compensated. In 2022, the average annual compensation of the top 10 CEOs in the U.S. was $156 million.[1] The ratio between the CEO's compensation and that of the typical employee in the same firm has increased from 20 in the 1970s to over 300 today—see Fig. 7.1. Translating this ratio of 300 to other human properties, such as intelligence or height, implies a person with an IQ of 30,000, or one who stands 1700 feet tall. Thus, top CEO compensation is extremely relative to some other human attributes. This may explain why CEO compensation is a topic of heated debate in the general public, as well as among academics.

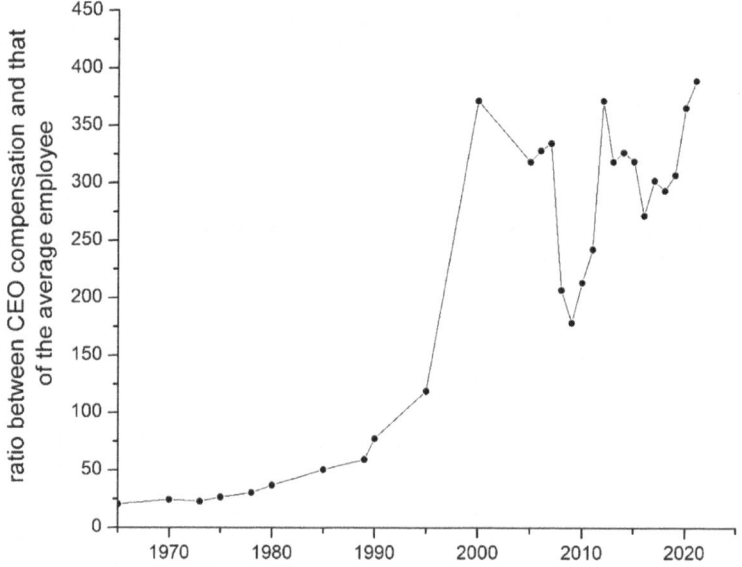

Fig. 7.1 The average ratio between the compensation of the CEO and the typical employee in the firm. The ratio is averaged across the 350 largest publicly traded U.S. firms. See Bivens and Kandra (2023) for detail

[1] https://www.cnbc.com/2023/07/05/heres-how-much-the-10-highest-paid-us-ceos-earn.html.

Some view CEO compensation as an equilibrium result of competition for scarce managerial talent (Axelson & Bond, 2015; Cremers & Grinstein, 2014; Gabaix & Landier, 2008; Hubbard, 2005; Oyer, 2004; Tervio, 2008). According to this view, if the CEO of a multi-billion firm can increase the company's bottom line by even only 1%, compensating this CEO by hundreds of millions of dollars is a good deal for the firm.

On the opposing side are those who view the dramatic increase in CEO compensation as a result of their increased negotiating power with complicit boards (Bebchuk & Fried, 2009; Bertrand & Mullainathan, 2001; Goergen & Renneboog, 2011; Newman & Mozes, 1999; Rappaport & Nodine, 1999; Tully, 1998).

Luck plays a key role in this debate. Bertrand and Mullainathan (2001) show that CEOs are sometimes rewarded for luck. Their classic example involves oil company CEOs whose compensations increase with the price of oil, which is, of course, a factor completely outside of their control. They've also shown that compensation is sensitive to other observable factors that are outside the control of the manager, such as exchange rates and industry shocks. Bertrand and Mullainathan conclude that "...CEO pay in fact responds as much to a lucky dollar as to a general dollar".

Levy (2016) estimates that as much as 90 cents of every dollar of CEO option compensation is actually paid for luck. Some schemes have been suggested to reduce compensation for luck, such as indexing options to the market return, or to the return of the firm's industry. Option indexing is rarely implemented, though, and it has only a limited effect in reducing compensation for luck. The reason is that luck is a fundamental and unavoidable property of investments. The following simple example illustrates this point.

Consider a risky project that requires an investment of $10 today, and yields either $16 or $6 next year, with equal probabilities. For the sake of simplicity, assume that the project's cost of capital is 0%.[2] Thus, the project has a positive NPV of $1,[3] and any good manager is supposed to accept it. When the manager takes this project, the firm value increases by the NPV of $1. When the future risky cashflow is realized, it represents either a positive or negative surprise relative to the expected cashflow

---

[2] Assuming a positive cost of capital has no substantial effect on the results, only makes the calculations a bit more cumbersome.

[3] $\text{NPV} = -10 + \frac{16+6}{2} = 1$.

value of \$11. If the realized cashflow is \$16, it represents a positive surprise of \$5, and the firm value increases by an additional \$5. Thus, in this case, the project has an aggregate effect of increasing the firm value by \$6. If the cashflow realized is only \$6, it represents a negative surprise of − \$5, and the firm value decreases by \$5 when it is realized. In this case, the project has an aggregate effect of decreasing the firm value by \$4 (+\$1 when the project is initially taken, and − \$5 when the disappointing cashflow is realized). Thus, the competent manager that accepts this positive NPV project has a 50% chance of ending up destroying firm value. If this happens, the board and other outside observers, who see only the negative bottom line, will not be very pleased with the manager, even though accepting the project was the correct decision a priori. It is fundamental property of our uncertain world that good *ex-ante* choices may lead to a bad *ex-post* outcomes.

In general, the more good choices the manager makes, the better the chances of creating value. Figure 7.2 shows the probability that the manager ends up destroying value as a function of the number of projects of the above type undertaken (assuming that the projects are independent). The jagged shape of the curve is due to the somewhat simplistic assumption of a binary outcome for the cashflow of each project.[4] Figure 7.3 shows the probability of destroying value as a result of accepting N good projects when the projects' cashflows are normally distributed, with the same parameters: each project has an NPV of \$1 and a standard deviation of \$5 of the future cashflow. The normal distribution of future cashflows is more realistic, and smoothens the curve. The main point is this: even if a manager makes $N = 5$ good decisions, the probability of destroying value (and possibly being terminated) is over 30%. Even if the manager undertakes $N = 10$ good projects, the probability is about 25% of destroying value.

An exact mirror image of this result holds for an incompetent manager who accepts bad projects. Consider the exact same project as before, but

---

[4] For example, if $N = 3$ projects are taken, there is a 50% of destroying value: the combinations ddd and ddu destroy value, while the combinations uuu and uud created value (where "u" denotes a realization of the high cashflow and "d" denotes a realization of the low cashflow. The ordering of outcomes is irrelevant). For $N = 5$, only the combinations ddddd and ddddu destroy value. There are 6 such combinations (with 5 different orderings of the u in the second case) out of the $2^5 = 32$ possible combinations, and the probability of value destruction is thus 18.75%.

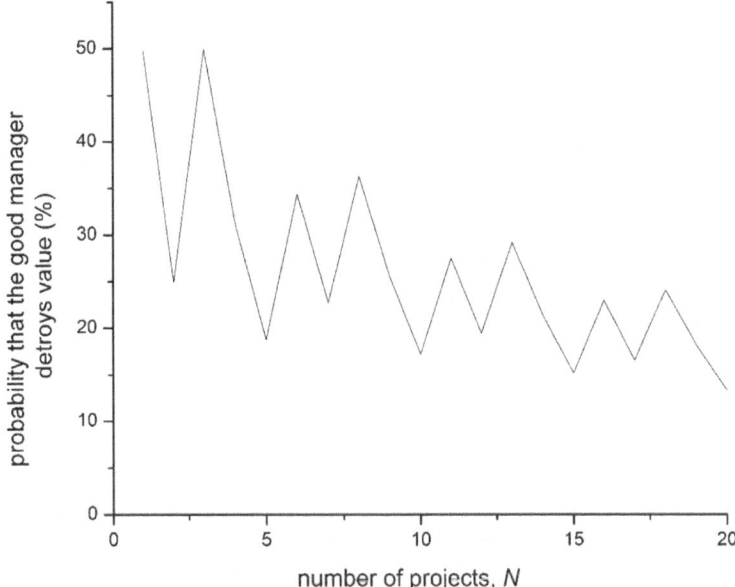

Fig. 7.2 The probability that a manager who accepts N independent projects with positive NPV ends up destroying value—a project with binary outcomes

with a required investment of $12, rather than $10. This project has an NPV of − $1, and should not be accepted. However, a manager accepting this project has a very good chance of ending up increasing firm value (50% in the binomial case, and about 42% in the normal case). Even a consistently bad manager who makes $N = 5$ bad decisions in a row has a probability exceeding 30% of ending up creating value.

Managers are typically hired and compensated based on their track records. Consider two managers, one making only good decisions (taking the positive NPV projects above), and the other making only bad decisions (taking only the negative NPV projects above). Figure 7.4 shows the probability that the bad manager ends up creating more value than the good manager, as a function of the number of projects that they take, N. A bad manager who makes 5 out of 5 bad decisions has a probability of about 25% of outperforming a good manager who makes 5 out of 5 good decisions.

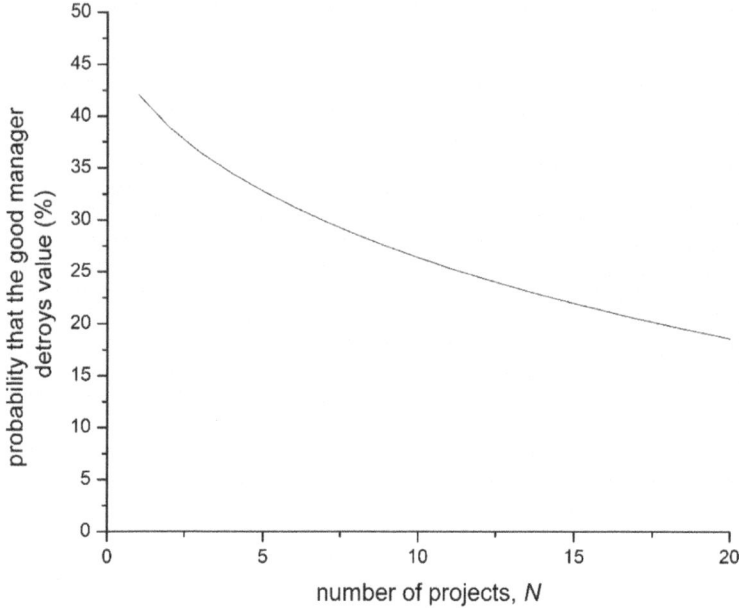

Fig. 7.3 The probability that a manager who accepts N independent projects with positive NPV ends up destroying value—a project with normally distributed outcomes

The role of luck depends on the "noise-to-signal" ratio, which can be captured by the standard deviation of cashflows divided by the project's NPV. This ratio depends on the project characteristics, and obviously varies across projects and industries.[5] Levy (2023) provides a very rough estimate of this ratio, based on empirical free cashflows of medium-sized firms, and finds an average ratio of 4.7. Thus, the above numerical examples, with a ratio of 5, may be not too far-fetched.

The emerging picture of the central role of luck in management may seem counter-intuitive. One reason is that we all know cases of very talented, ambitious, and hard-working individuals who created billion-dollar empires from scratch. These managers' stories are inspiring, but they represent a very biased sample. For each such successful manager,

[5] Note that the noise-to-signal ratio may be reduced by investing in information acquisition.

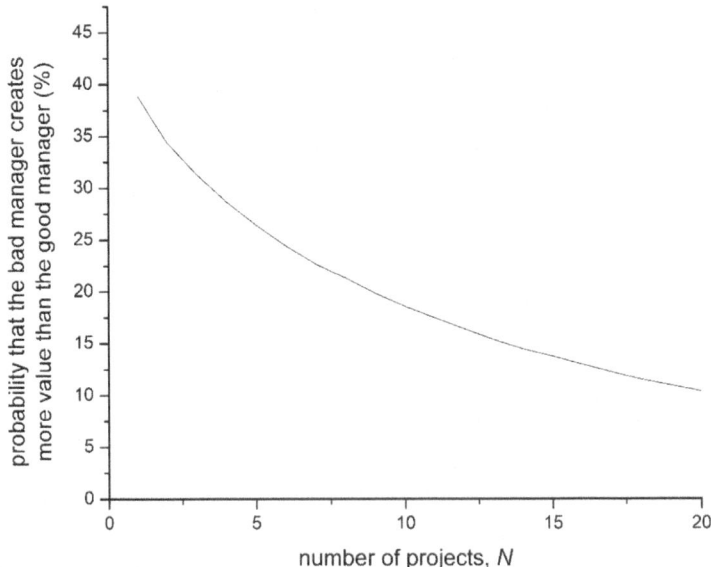

Fig. 7.4 The probability that a bad manager who accepts N negative-NPV projects ends up creating more value than a good manager who accepts N positive-NPV projects

there are probably hundreds of managers, who are just as talented and hard-working, but did not succeed. Thus, the successful managers are not *only* talented and hard-working, they are probably also very *lucky*, a point made very convincingly by Frank (2016).

7.2   The Role of Luck in Investments and the Wealth Distribution

In any given year, many investors obtain returns higher than that of the market. Some of them may have exceptional investment skills, while others may have just been lucky. How can we distinguish between investment skill and luck? A natural way would be to look at persistence over time: an investor who keeps beating the market year after year is likely to be skilled, while another who beats the market in 1 year but does poorly in the next years seems to have been just lucky in that particular year. Samuelson (1989) summarizes the empirical research on the persistence of investment performance, writing:

> Those lucky money managers who happen in any period to beat the comprehensive averages in total return seem primarily to have been merely lucky. Being on the honor roll in 1974 does not make you appreciably more likely to be on the 1975 honor roll." (p. 4).

There are a handful of investors who have been able to consistently beat the market for decades. They are generally perceived as possessing exceptional talent, and have gained fame and recognition. Skeptics, however, claim that a few such exceptional track records are to be expected even under a pure luck model. The chances of throwing 20 heads in a row are about 1 in a million. Thus, if a few million investors are flipping coins randomly, a handful are expected to get 20 heads in a row.

While it is difficult to determine whether a specific investor is talented or lucky (or more precisely, what are the relative weights of these two factors in the investor's performance), looking at the distribution of all investors' performances can shed light on the relative importance of luck. If one has data on the investment performance of all investors in every year, this could be examined directly. But such data is typically unavailable. One indirect way to investigate the issue is by looking at the distribution of wealth among the rich. At low and intermediate levels of wealth, the primary factors for changes in wealth are labor income and consumption. However, for the rich, changes in wealth are primarily driven by investment outcomes. Thus, looking at the top end of the wealth distribution may be informative about talent differences in investments.

Empirically, the wealth distribution at the top end (right tail) closely follows a power-law, or Pareto, distribution (Pareto 1897; Steindl, 1965; Atkinson & Harrison, 1978; Persky, 1992; Levy & Solomon, 1997). Figure 7.5, for example, shows the wealth of the 1000 wealthiest individuals in the U.S. in 2023 as a function of their rank, as reported by the Forbes "rich list". A power-law distribution predicts a negative linear relation between wealth and rank, when plotted on a log–log scale (Takayasu, 1990). Figure 7.5 shows that the empirical distribution is in excellent agreement with this prediction.

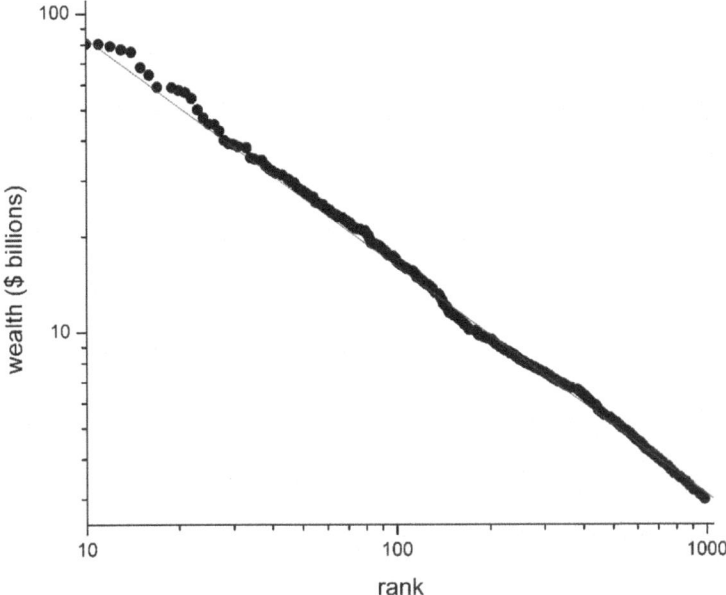

Fig. 7.5 The wealth of the richest individuals in the U.S. as a function of their rank in the wealth ranking (log–log scale). The data is from the Forbes 2023 "rich list" (https://app.gigasheet.com/spreadsheet/forbes-billionaires-evolution-1997-2023). A power-law wealth distribution implies a negative linear relationship. The empirical data are in excellent agreement with this prediction

What can this empirical regularity teach us about the role of luck in investments? Levy (2003) proves that an investment process where all investors are equally talented, and differ only in their luck, leads to a power-law wealth distribution.[6] Thus, the empirical distribution is consistent with a process where differences in investment outcomes are entirely due to luck. Moreover, if there are systematic differences in talent, i.e. there are talented investors who draw returns for a distribution with a

---

[6] The model also assumes that there is a minimal wealth level required to participate in the investment process. When an investor's wealth falls below this level, the investor is excluded, and a new investor enters, with the minimum wealth level. Thus, wealth follows a random multiplicative process with a lower bound, which leads to a steady-state power-law distribution (Furstenberg, 1965; Levy, 2003).

higher mean than that of "typical" investors, the resulting wealth distribution is systematically different than the power-law distribution. The larger the difference between the mean return of the talented investors and the mean return of the typical investors, the larger the deviation of the wealth distribution from the power-law distribution. Levy and Levy (2003) employ this observation to estimate an upper bound on the differences in investment talent. They conclude that to be consistent with the empirical wealth distribution, the mean returns of the most talented investors can exceed those of typical investors by at most 1%, on an annual basis.

What does a difference of 1% in talent imply about the relative importance of talent and luck? One question we can examine is the following: what are the chances that a "typical" investor ends up doing better than the talented investor? Fig. 7.6 shows the answer, as a function of the number of investment years. The typical investor is assumed to draw rates of return from a distribution with a mean of 10% and a standard deviation of 20% (these figures are close to the historical annual return parameters of the S&P 500 index). The talented investor is assumed to draw returns independently from a distribution with the same standard deviation, but a mean that is 1% higher, i.e. a mean of 11%. Figure 7.6 shows that even after 20 years, the typical investor has a 44% chance of ending up wealthier than the talented investor.

Another issue we can examine is to what extent talented investors "surface to the top". For example, suppose that we have a large population of investors, half typical and half normal, with the parameters discussed above. If we look at the most successful (i.e. wealthiest) investors, what would be the share of typical investors among them? Fig. 7.7 shows the answer, as a function of the number of investment years. The figure shows that even after 20 years, about 41% of the top 10% of investors will be typical (and 59% will be talented). These proportions are not all that different than their 50–50% proportions in the total population. The share of typical investors among the top 2% of most successful investors is a bit lower, but it is still about 38% even after 20 years.

These results suggest that luck plays a central role in investments. Again, this may be hard to accept, especially for those at the top of the wealth distribution (more on this in the next section). But this conclusion resonates with the words attributed to King Solomon, credited as being "the wisest of all men":

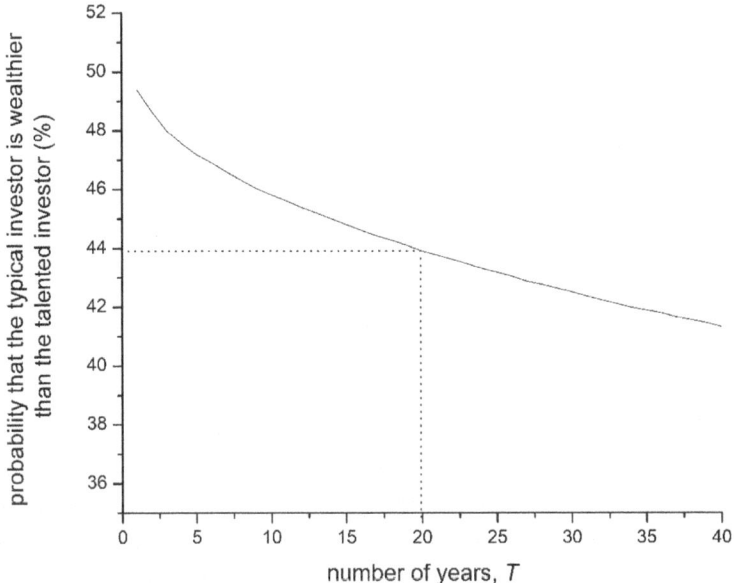

Fig. 7.6 The probability of a typical investor ending up with higher wealth than a talented investor as a function of the number of investment years. Both investors have the same standard deviation of returns (20%), but the talented investor has a mean return 1% higher than the typical investor (11% and 10%, respectively)

> I returned and saw under the sun, that the race is not to the swift, nor the battle to the strong, neither yet bread to the wise, nor yet riches to men of understanding, nor yet favor to men of skill, but time and chance happeneth to them all. (Ecclesiastes 9:11)

7.3   Luck and Mutual Funds Selection

Luck has important implications both for investors selecting mutual funds and for fund managers. Luck, i.e. randomness, is closely tied to the issue of estimation error and to the difficulty of predicting future performance. A good fund with a high ex-ante Sharpe ratio may very well end up having lower ex-post performance relative to a mediocre fund with a lower ex-ante Sharpe ratio. The shrinkage method suggested in Chapter 4

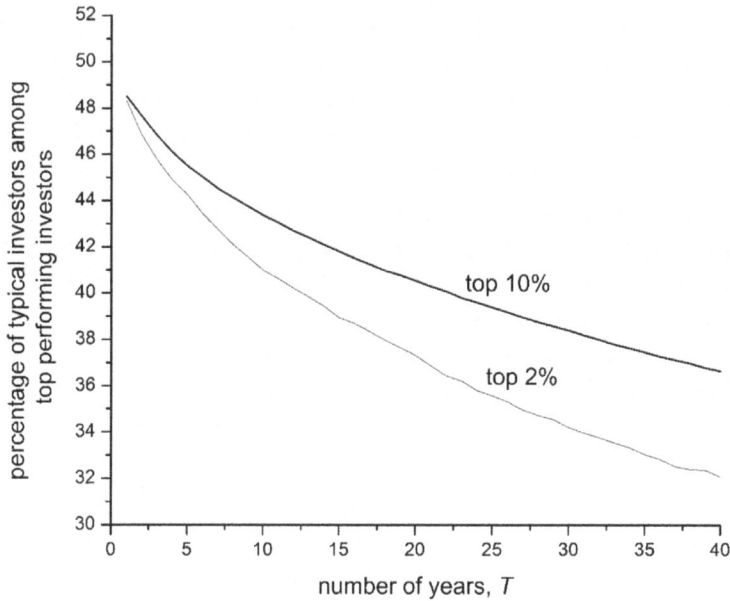

Fig. 7.7 The proportion of typical investors among the most successful 10% and 2% of investors. The entire population consists of the same number of talented and typical investors

takes estimation error into account, and helps in identifying better funds. This leads to better performance, on average, as discussed in Chapter 4. However, investors should have realistic expectations: even if one applies state-of-the-art methods for fund selection, this does not guarantee good performance. Just like the talented investor who has a substantial probability of underperforming relative to a typical investor, a well-informed investor, who is able to identify the fund that is ex-ante better, has a rather high probability of underperforming relative to an un-informed investor selecting a fund with worse ex-ante parameters. Informed fund selection leads to better performance *on average*, and is economically valuable, but this is very different than guaranteeing better performance in every period.

A talented and hard-working fund manager who is able to achieve better-than-average ex-ante performance should also realize that this will not necessarily imply good realized performance. This is similar to the CEO making good decisions or the investor making good choices, who may face disappointing results. However, the talented fund manager can increase his probability of beating the benchmark by increasing the correlation between the fund and the benchmark returns. For example, consider a fund manager who has the S&P 500 as a benchmark. Assume that the S&P returns are drawn from a normal distribution with a mean of 10% and a standard deviation of 20%. Consider a talented manager who is able to achieve superior ex-ante performance, with the same standard deviation of 20% but a higher mean of 11%. Figure 7.8 shows the manager's probability of beating the benchmark, as a function of the number of investment periods. If the fund's returns are independent of the benchmark's, the probability that the talented manager beats the index is rather modest (this is just the mirror image of Fig. 7.6). However, the higher the correlation with the benchmark, the higher the manager's probability of beating it. In the extreme case of perfect correlation, the fund yields a return 1% higher than the benchmark's in each and every period, and over-performance is guaranteed. Thus, even though correlation with the benchmark does not affect the fund's Sharpe ratio, it has a large impact on the probability of beating it. For example, if the manager is able to increase the correlation with the benchmark from $\rho = 0.5$ to $\rho = 0.9$, keeping all other parameters constant, the probability of beating the benchmark after 20 periods increases from about 57% to about 69%.[7]

The way fund managers perceive luck may affect their behavior and subsequent performance. Wang (2023) shows that, like most other people, fund managers exhibit a self-attribution bias: they tend to attribute good performance to their own actions, and to attribute bad performance to luck (see also Taleb, 2016). This is nicely captured in Wang's paper titled: "Heads I win, tails it's chance". Moreover, the managers with the strongest self-attribution bias tend to engage in excessive trading in the following period, perhaps because of a boost to their overconfidence, and this in turn tends to negatively affect future fund

---

[7] This is closely related to the typical mandate given to fund managers by institutions: for a given average tracking error relative to a benchmark, minimize tracking error volatility. Roll (1992) shows that this mandate motivates managers to select inefficient mean–variance portfolios with inferior Sharpe ratios. The difference between the two frameworks is that here we take the fund's mean return and standard deviation as given, while in the tracking error framework the portfolio parameters change with the designated average tracking error.

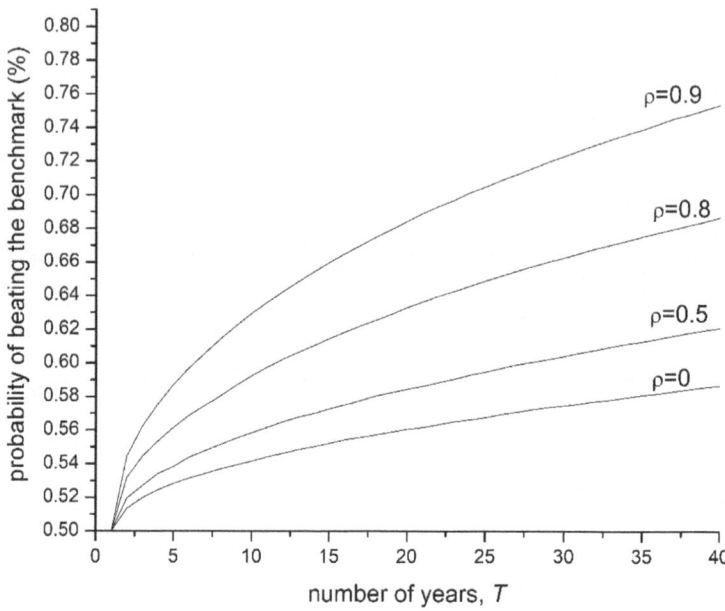

Fig. 7.8 The probability that a talented fund manager beats the benchmark, as a function of the number of investment years, and the fund's correlation with the benchmark. The fund and the benchmark have the same volatility, but the fund's expected return is 1% higher. Even with a correlation of 0.9 and 20 years of investment, the probability that the manager beats the benchmark ex-post is less than 70%

performance. Thus, managers who are more realistic in their perceptions of the role of luck, especially after a realization of good luck, tend to subsequently trade less and perform better.

7.4   Summary

Most of us tend to underestimate the importance of luck. This may be a bias hard-wired by evolution: acknowledging the importance of luck may discourage exerting effort, and could thus be detrimental (Frank, 2016; Johnson & Fowler, 2011; Weiner, 1985). On the other hand, a realistic perspective about the role of luck is important in the realm of investments. It tells investors what can, and what cannot, be expected from informed mutual fund selection. It is also important for mutual fund managers. They should realize that even if they are talented and do everything right, there is a substantial chance they'll end up under-performing relative to their benchmark. They can improve their chances, though, by increasing their correlation with the benchmark. Like all humans, mutual fund managers tend to attribute good performance to their effort and skill, and bad performance to bad luck. This typically leads to overconfidence, excessive trading, and on average, hinders subsequent performance. A realistic view regarding the importance of luck may help fund managers resist this bias, and improve their performance.

Fortune favors the lucky.

Reproduced from Tom Weller's "Minims": https://tweller.com/minims/index.html

REFERENCES

Atkinson, A. B., & Harrison, A. J. (1978). *Distribution of personal wealth in Britain*. Cambridge University Press.

Axelson, U., & Bond, P. (2015). Wall street occupations. *The Journal of Finance, 70*(5), 1949–1996.

Bebchuk, L. A., & Fried, J. M. (2009). *Pay without performance: The unfulfilled promise of executive compensation*. Harvard University Press.

Bertrand, M., & Mullainathan, S. (2001). Are CEOs rewarded for luck? The ones without principals are. *The Quarterly Journal of Economics, 116*(3), 901–932.

Bivens, J., & Kandra, J. (2023). *CEO pay slightly declined in 2022*. Economic Policy Institute Report.

Cremers, K. M., & Grinstein, Y. (2014). Does the market for CEO talent explain controversial CEO pay practices? *Review of Finance, 18*(3), 921–960.

Frank, R. H. (2016). *Success and luck: Good fortune and the myth of meritocracy*. Princeton University Press.

Furstenberg, H. (1965). Translation-invariant cones of functions on semi-simple lie groups. *Bulletin of the American Mathematical Society, 71*(2), 271–326.

Gabaix, X., & Landier, A. (2008). Why has CEO pay increased so much? *The Quarterly Journal of Economics, 123*(1), 49–100.

Goergen, M., & Renneboog, L. (2011). Managerial compensation. *Journal of Corporate Finance, 17*(4), 1068–1077.

Hubbard, R. G. (2005). Pay without performance: A market equilibrium critique. *Journal of Corporation Law, 30*(4), 717.

Johnson, D. D., & Fowler, J. H. (2011). The evolution of overconfidence. *Nature, 477*(7364), 317–320.

Levy, M. (2016). *90 cents of every 'pay-for-performance' dollar are paid for luck*. https://corpgov.law.harvard.edu/2016/09/29/90-cents-of-every-pay-for-performance-dollar-are-paid-for-luck/

Levy, M. (2003). Are rich people smarter? *Journal of Economic Theory, 110*(1), 42–64.

Levy, H. (2016). *Stochastic dominance: Investment decision making under uncertainty*. Springer.

Levy, M., & Levy, H. (2003). Investment talent and the Pareto wealth distribution: Theoretical and experimental analysis. *Review of Economics and Statistics, 85*(3), 709–725.

Levy, M. (2023). *Projects with no cost of capital*. Hebrew University working paper.

Levy, M., & Solomon, S. (1997). New evidence for the power-law distribution of wealth. *Physica a: Statistical Mechanics and Its Applications, 242*(1–2), 90–94.

Newman, H. A., & Mozes, H. A. (1999). Does the composition of the compensation committee influence CEO compensation practices? *Financial Management, 1999*, 41–53.

Oyer, P. (2004). Why do firms use incentives that have no incentive effects? *The Journal of Finance, 59*(4), 1619–1650.

Pareto, V. (1897). *Cours d'economique politique* (Vol. 2). Lausanne: Rouge.

Persky, J. (1992). Retrospectives: Pareto's law. *Journal of Economic Perspectives, 6*(2), 181–192.

Rappaport, A., & Nodine, T. (1999). New thinking on how to link executive pay with performance. *Harvard Business Review, 77*(2), 91–92.

Roll, R. (1992). A mean/variance analysis of tracking error. *Journal of Portfolio Management, 18*(4), 13.

Samuelson, P. A. (1989). The judgement of economic science on rational portfolio man. *Journal of Portfolio Management, 16*(1), 4.

Steindl, J. (1965). *Random processes and the growth of firms: A study of the Pareto law*. Charles Griffin & Company.

Takayasu, H. (1990). *Fractals in the physical sciences*. Manchester University Press.

Taleb, N. N. (2016). *Fooled by randomness: The hidden role of chance in life and in the markets*. Editeurs Divers USA.

Tervio, M. (2008). The difference that CEOs make: An assignment model approach. *American Economic Review, 98*(3), 642–668.

Tully, S. (1998). Raising the bar. *Fortune, 137*, 134–138.

Wang, M. (2023). *Heads I win, tails it's chance: Mutual fund performance self-attribution*. Working paper.

Weiner, B. (1985). An attributional theory of achievement motivation and emotion. *Psychological Review, 92*(4), 548.

REFERENCES

Agnew, J. R., Anderson, L. R., Gerlach, J. R., & Szykman, L. R. (2008). Who chooses annuities? An experimental investigation of the role of gender, framing, and defaults. *American Economic Review, 98*(2), 418–422.

Aitchison, J., & Brown, J. A. (1957). *The lognormal distribution with special reference to its uses in economics*. Cambridge University Press.

Almazan, A., Brown, K. C., Carlson, M., & Chapman, D. A. (2004). Why constrain your mutual fund manager? *Journal of Financial Economics, 73*(2), 289–321.

Amihud, Y., & Goyenko, R. (2013). Mutual fund's R^2 as predictor of performance. *The Review of Financial Studies, 26*(3), 667–694.

Andreoni, J., & Sprenger, C. (2012). Estimating time preferences from convex budgets. *American Economic Review, 102*(7), 3333–3356.

Arrow, K. J. (1971). *Essays in the theory of risk-bearing*. North-Holland Pub. Co.

Atkinson, A. B., & Harrison, A. J. (1978). *Distribution of personal wealth in Britain*. Cambridge University Press.

Axelson, U., & Bond, P. (2015). Wall street occupations. *The Journal of Finance, 70*(5), 1949–1996.

Baks, K. P., Metrick, A., & Wachter, J. (2001). Should investors avoid all actively managed mutual funds? A study in Bayesian performance evaluation. *The Journal of Finance, 56*(1), 45–85.

Barber, B. M., Odean, T., Zheng, L. (2000). *The behavior of mutual fund investors*. Unpublished working paper.

Barber, B. M., Huang, X., & Odean, T. (2016). Which factors matter to investors? Evidence from mutual fund flows. *The Review of Financial Studies, 29*(10), 2600–2642.

Barber, B. M., Odean, T., & Zheng, L. (2005). Out of sight, out of mind: The effects of expenses on mutual fund flows. *The Journal of Business, 78*(6), 2095–2120.

Barras, L., Gagliardini, P., & Scaillet, O. (2022). Skill, scale, and value creation in the mutual fund industry. *The Journal of Finance, 77*(1), 601–638.

Barro, R. J., & Jin, T. (2011). On the size distribution of macroeconomic disasters. *Econometrica, 79*(5), 1567–1589.

Bayes, T. (1763). LII. An essay towards solving a problem in the doctrine of chances. By the late Rev. Mr. Bayes, FRS communicated by Mr. Price, in a letter to John Canton, AMFR S. *Philosophical Transactions of the Royal Society of London, 53,* 370–418.

Bebchuk, L. A., & Fried, J. M. (2003). Executive compensation as an agency problem. *Journal of Economic Perspectives, 17*(3), 71–92.

Bebchuk, L. A., & Fried, J. M. (2009). *Pay without performance: The unfulfilled promise of executive compensation.* Harvard University Press.

Bem, D. J. (1965). An experimental analysis of self-persuasion. *Journal of Experimental Social Psychology, 1*(3), 199–218.

Ben-David, I., Li, J., Rossi, A., & Song, Y. (2022). What do mutual fund investors really care about? *The Review of Financial Studies, 35*(4), 1723–1774.

Berk, J. B. (1997). Necessary conditions for the CAPM. *Journal of Economic Theory, 73*(1), 245–257.

Berk, J. B., & Green, R. C. (2004). Mutual fund flows and performance in rational markets. *Journal of Political Economy, 112*(6), 1269–1295.

Berk, J. B., & van Binsbergen, J. H. (2015). Measuring skill in the mutual fund industry. *Journal of Financial Economics, 118*(1), 1–20.

Bernoulli, D. (1738). 'Specimen theoriae novae de mensura sortis,' in Commentarii Academiae Scientiarum Imperialis Petropolitanae, vol. 5. English translation by Louise Sommer with notes by Karl Menger, 'Exposition of a new theory on the measurement of risk,' Papers of the Imperial Academy of Sciences in Petersburg. *Econometrica, 1954,* 23–26.

Bernstein, P. L. (1976). The time of your life. *The Journal of Portfolio Management, 2*(4), 4.

Bernstein, P. L. (2006). The paradox of the efficient market. *Journal of Portfolio Management, 32*(2), 1.

Bertrand, M., & Mullainathan, S. (2001). Are CEOs rewarded for luck? The ones without principals are. *The Quarterly Journal of Economics, 116*(3), 901–932.

Billingsley, P. (2008). *Probability and measure.* Wiley.

Bivens, J., & Kandra, J. (2023). *CEO pay slightly declined in 2022.* Economic Policy Institute Report.

Black, F. (1972). Capital market equilibrium with restricted borrowing. *The Journal of Business, 45*(3), 444–455.

Blake, D., Caulfield, T., Ioannidis, C., & Tonks, I. (2017). New evidence on mutual fund performance: A comparison of alternative bootstrap methods. *Journal of Financial and Quantitative Analysis, 2017*, 1–21.

Blume, M. E., & Friend, I. (1975). The asset structure of individual portfolios and some implications for utility functions. *The Journal of Finance, 30*(2), 585–603.

Bodnaruk, A., & Simonov, A. (2016). Loss-averse preferences, performance, and career success of institutional investors. *The Review of Financial Studies, 29*(11), 3140–3176.

Bogan, V. (2008). Stock market participation and the internet. *Journal of Financial and Quantitative Analysis, 43*(1), 191–211.

Bollen, N. P., & Busse, J. A. (2001). On the timing ability of mutual fund managers. *The Journal of Finance, 56*(3), 1075–1094.

Bradley, R. C. (2007). *Introduction to strong mixing conditions*. LOndon: Kendrick Press.

Breiman, L. (1960). Investment policies for expanding businesses optimal in a long-run sense. *Naval Research Logistics Quarterly, 7*(4), 647–651.

Brown, K. C., Harlow, W. V., & Starks, L. T. (1996). Of tournaments and temptations: An analysis of managerial incentives in the mutual fund industry. *The Journal of Finance, 51*(1), 85–110.

Browning, E. K. (1976). The marginal cost of public funds. *Journal of Political Economy, 84*(2), 283–298.

Brunnermeier, M. K., & Nagel, S. (2008). Do wealth fluctuations generate time-varying risk aversion? Micro-evidence on individuals' asset allocation. *American Economic Review, 98*(3), 713–736.

Carhart, M. M. (1997). On persistence in mutual fund performance. *The Journal of Finance, 52*(1), 57–82.

Chamberlain, G. (1983). A Characterization of the distributions that imply mean-variance utility functions. *Journal of Economic Theory, 29*, 185–201.

Chevalier, J., & Ellison, G. (1997). Risk taking by mutual funds as a response to incentives. *Journal of Political Economy, 105*(6), 1167–1200.

Chevalier, J., & Ellison, G. (1999a). Are some mutual fund managers better than others? Cross-sectional patterns in behavior and performance. *The Journal of Finance, 54*(3), 875–899.

Chevalier, J., & Ellison, G. (1999b). Career concerns of mutual fund managers. *The Quarterly Journal of Economics, 114*(2), 389–432.

Chiappori, P. A., & Paiella, M. (2011). Relative risk aversion is constant: Evidence from panel data. *Journal of the European Economic Association, 9*(6), 1021–1052.

Cremers, K. M., & Grinstein, Y. (2014). Does the market for CEO talent explain controversial CEO pay practices? *Review of Finance, 18*(3), 921–960.

Cremers, K. M., & Petajisto, A. (2009). How active is your fund manager? A new measure that predicts performance. *The Review of Financial Studies, 22*(9), 3329–3365.

Daniel, K., Grinblatt, M., Titman, S., & Wermers, R. (1997). Measuring mutual fund performance with characteristic-based benchmarks. *The Journal of Finance, 52*(3), 1035–1058.

Daniel, K., Hirshleifer, D., & Subrahmanyam, A. (1998). Investor psychology and security market under-and overreactions. *Journal of Finance, 1998,* 1839–1885.

De Bondt, W. F., & Thaler, R. H. (1990). Do security analysts overreact? *The American Economic Review, 1990,* 52–57.

De Mel, S., McKenzie, D., & Woodruff, C. (2008). Returns to capital in microenterprises: Evidence from a field experiment. *The Quarterly Journal of Economics, 123*(4), 1329–1372.

Del Guercio, D., & Reuter, J. (2014). Mutual fund performance and the incentive to generate alpha. *The Journal of Finance, 69*(4), 1673–1704.

Del Guercio, D., & Tkac, P. A. (2008). Star power: The effect of Monrningstar ratings on mutual fund flow. *Journal of Financial and Quantitative Analysis, 43*(4), 907–936.

Dolde, W., & Tobin, J. (1971). *Wealth, liquidity, and consumption* (No. 311). Cowles Foundation for Research in Economics, Yale University.

Durrett, R. (2019). *Probability: Theory and examples* (Vol. 49). London: Cambridge University Press.

Dybvig, P. H., & Ross, S. A. (1985). Differential information and performance measurement using a security market line. *The Journal of Finance, 40*(2), 383–399.

Evans, R. B. (2010). Mutual fund incubation. *The Journal of Finance, 65*(4), 1581–1611.

Fama, E. F. (1965). The behavior of stock-market prices. *The Journal of Business, 38*(1), 34–105.

Fama, E. F. (1970). Efficient capital markets: A review of theory and empirical work. *The Journal of Finance, 25*(2), 383–417.

Fama, E. F., & French, K. R. (1992). The cross-section of expected stock returns. *The Journal of Finance, 47*(2), 427–465.

Fama, E. F., & French, K. R. (1993). Common risk factors in the returns on stocks and bonds. *Journal of Financial Economics, 33*(1), 3–56.

Fama, E. F., & French, K. R. (1995). Size and book-to-market factors in earnings and returns. *The Journal of Finance, 50*(1), 131–155.

Fama, E. F., & French, K. R. (2010). Luck versus skill in the cross-section of mutual fund returns. *The Journal of Finance, 65*(5), 1915–1947.

Fama, E. F., & French, K. R. (2015). A five-factor asset pricing model. *Journal of Financial Economics, 116*(1), 1–22.

Ferson, W. E., & Schadt, R. W. (1996). Measuring fund strategy and performance in changing economic conditions. *The Journal of Finance, 51*(2), 425–461.

Fischer, H. (2011). *A history of the central limit theorem: From classical to modern probability theory* (Vol. 4). Springer.

Fishburn, P. C. (1974). Convex stochastic dominance with continuous distribution functions. *Journal of Economic Theory, 7*(2), 143–158.

Fortune, P. (2000). Margin requirements, margin loans, and margin rates: Practice and principles. *New England Economic Review, 19*, 1.

Frank, R. H. (2016). *Success and luck: Good fortune and the myth of meritocracy.* London: Princeton University Press.

Friend, I., & Blume, M. E. (1975). The demand for risky assets. *The American Economic Review, 65*(5), 900–922.

Furstenberg, H. (1965). Translation-invariant cones of functions on semi-simple lie groups. *Bulletin of the American Mathematical Society, 71*(2), 271–326.

Gabaix, X., & Landier, A. (2008). Why has CEO pay increased so much? *The Quarterly Journal of Economics, 123*(1), 49–100.

Galton, F. (1907). Vox Populi. *Nature, 75*, 450–451.

Garleanu, N., & Pedersen, L. H. (2019). *Active and passive investing.* Available at SSRN 3253537.

Gil-Bazo, J., & Ruiz-Verdú, P. (2009). The relation between price and performance in the mutual fund industry. *The Journal of Finance, 64*(5), 2153–2183.

Gilovich, T., Vallone, R., & Tversky, A. (1985). The hot hand in basketball: On the misperception of random sequences. *Cognitive Psychology, 17*(3), 295–314.

Goergen, M., & Renneboog, L. (2011). Managerial compensation. *Journal of Corporate Finance, 17*(4), 1068–1077.

Grinblatt, M., & Titman, S. (1989). Mutual fund performance: An analysis of quarterly portfolio holdings. *Journal of Business, 1989*, 393–416.

Grossman, S. J., & Stiglitz, J. E. (1980). On the impossibility of informationally efficient markets. *The American Economic Review, 70*(3), 393–408.

Gruber, M. J. (1996). Another puzzle: The growth in actively managed mutual funds. *The Journal of Finance, 51*(3), 783–810.

Hadar, J., & Russell, W. R. (1969). Rules for ordering uncertain prospects. *The American Economic Review, 59*(1), 25–34.

Hakansson, N. H. (1970). Optimal investment and consumption strategies under risk for a class of utility functions. *Econometrica, 38*, 587–607.

Hakansson, N. H. (1971). Multi-period mean-variance analysis: Toward a general theory of portfolio choice. *The Journal of Finance, 26*(4), 857–884.

Hanoch, G., & Levy, H. (1969). The efficiency analysis of choices involving risk. *Review of Economic Studies, 36*(3), 335–346.

Hansen, L. P., & Singleton, K. J. (1982). Generalized instrumental variables estimation of nonlinear rational expectations models. *Econometrica, 50*(5), 1269–1286.

Harvey, C. R., & Liu, Y. (2018). Detecting repeatable performance. *The Review of Financial Studies, 31*(7), 2499–2552.

Harvey, C. R., & Liu, Y. (2022). Luck versus skill in the cross section of mutual fund returns: Reexamining the evidence. *The Journal of Finance, 77*(3), 1921–1966.

Heinemann, F. (2008). Measuring risk aversion and the wealth effect. In *Risk aversion in experiments*. Emerald Group Publishing Limited.

Hubbard, R. G. (2005). Pay without performance: A market equilibrium critique. *Journal of Corporation Law, 30*(4), 717.

Ibbotson Associates Research Paper—Lifetime Asset Allocations: Methodologies for target maturity funds (2008). https://corporate.morningstar.com/ib/documents/MethodologyDocuments/IBBAssociates/LifetimeAssetAllocMeth021108.pdf

Investment Company Institute (ICI). (2023). Factbook: https://www.ici.org/system/files/2023-05/2023-factbook.pdf

James, W., & Stein, C. (1961). Estimation with quadratic loss. In *Proceedings of the 4th Berkeley symposium on mathematical statistics and probability, Volume 1: Contributions to the theory of statistics*.

Jensen, M. C. (1968). The performance of mutual funds in the period 1945–1964. *The Journal of Finance, 23*(2), 389–416.

Johnson, D. D., & Fowler, J. H. (2011). The evolution of overconfidence. *Nature, 477*(7364), 317–320.

Jones, M. A., & Smythe, T. (2003). The information content of mutual fund print advertising. *Journal of Consumer Affairs, 37*(1), 22–41.

Jorion, P. (1986). Bayes–Stein estimation for portfolio analysis. *Journal of Financial and Quantitative Analysis, 21*(3), 279–292.

Kahneman, D., & Tversky, A. (1979). Prospect theory: An analysis of decision under risk. *Econometrica, 47*(2), 263–292.

Kaniel, R., & Parham, R. (2017). WSJ Category Kings—The impact of media attention on consumer and mutual fund investment decisions. *Journal of Financial Economics, 123*(2), 337–356.

Kelly, J. L. (1956). A new interpretation of information rate. *The Bell System Technical Journal, 35*(4), 917–926.

Khorana, A., Servaes, H., & Wedge, L. (2007). Portfolio manager ownership and fund performance. *Journal of Financial Economics, 85*(1), 179–204.

Kinnel, R. (2010). *How expense ratios and star ratings predict success*. https://www.morningstar.com/articles/347327/article

Kosowski, R., Timmermann, A., Wermers, R., & White, H. (2006). Can mutual fund "stars" really pick stocks? New evidence from a bootstrap analysis. *The Journal of Finance, 61*(6), 2551–2595.

Kroll, Y., Levy, H., & Markowitz, H. M. (1984). Mean-variance versus direct utility maximization. *The Journal of Finance, 39*(1), 47–61.

Kydland, F. E., & Prescott, E. C. (1982). Time to build and aggregate fluctuations. *Econometrica: Journal of the Econometric Society*, 1345–1370.

Latane, H. A. (1959). Criteria for choice among risky ventures. *Journal of Political Economy, 67*(2), 144–155.

Lee, P. M. (2012). *Bayesian statistics*. Oxford University Press.

Leippold, M., & Rueegg, R. (2020). How rational and competitive is the market for mutual funds? *Review of Finance, 24*(3), 579–613.

Leland, H. E. (1969). Dynamic portfolio theory. *The Journal of Finance, 24*(3), 543–544.

Levhari, D., & Levy, H. (1977). The capital asset pricing model and the investment horizon. *The Review of Economics and Statistics, 1977*, 92–104.

Levi, Y., & Welch, I. (2017). Best practice for cost-of-capital estimates. *Journal of Financial and Quantitative Analysis, 52*(2), 427–463.

Levy, H. (1972). Portfolio performance and the investment horizon. *Management Science, 18*(12), B-645.

Levy, H. (1973a). Stochastic dominance among lognormal prospects. *International Economic Review, 1973*, 601–614.

Levy, H. (1973b). Stochastic dominance, efficiency criteria, and efficient portfolios: The multi-period case. *The American Economic Review, 63*(5), 986–994.

Levy, H. (1991). The mean-coefficient-of-variation rule: The lognormal case. *Management Science, 37*(6), 745–747.

Levy, H. (1994). Absolute and relative risk aversion: An experimental study. *Journal of Risk and Uncertainty, 8*, 289–307.

Levy, H. (2015). Aging population, retirement, and risk taking. *Management Science, 62*(5), 1415–1430.

Levy, H. (2016a). *Stochastic dominance: Investment decision making under uncertainty*. Springer.

Levy, H., De Giorgi, E. G., & Hens, T. (2012). Two paradigms and Nobel prizes in economics: A contradiction or coexistence? *European Financial Management, 18*(2), 163–182.

Levy, H., & Duchin, R. (2004). Asset return distributions and the investment horizon. *Journal of Portfolio Management, 30*(3), 47.

Levy, H., & Levy, M. (2004). Prospect theory and mean-variance analysis. *Review of Financial Studies, 17*(4), 1015–1041.

Levy, H., & Levy, M. (2021a). The cost of diversification over time, and a simple way to improve target-date funds. *Journal of Banking and Finance, 122*, 105995.

Levy, H., & Levy, M. (2021b). Prospect theory, constant relative risk aversion, and the investment horizon. *PLoS ONE, 16*(4), e0248904.

Levy, H., & Markowitz, H. M. (1979). Approximating expected utility by a function of mean and variance. *The American Economic Review, 69*(3), 308–317.

Levy, H., & Sarnat, M. (1994). *Capital investment and financial decisions.* Pearson Education.

Levy, M. (2003). Are rich people smarter? *Journal of Economic Theory, 110*(1), 42–64.

Levy, M. (2016). *90 cents of every 'pay-for-performance' dollar are paid for luck.* https://corpgov.law.harvard.edu/2016/09/29/90-cents-of-every-pay-for-performance-dollar-are-paid-for-luck/

Levy, M. (2023a). The deadweight loss of active management. *The Journal of Investing, 32,* 17–41.

Levy, M. (2023b). The cost of investment hubris. *Journal of Portfolio Management, 50*(1), 1–16.

Levy, M. (2023c). *Projects with no cost of capital.* Hebrew University working paper.

Levy, M., (2024a). *Mutual fund selection and the investment horizon.* Hebrew University working paper.

Levy, M. (2024b). Relative risk aversion must be close to 1. *Annals of Operations Research, 2024,* 1.

Levy, M., & Levy, H. (2003). Investment talent and the Pareto wealth distribution: Theoretical and experimental analysis. *Review of Economics and Statistics, 85*(3), 709–725.

Levy, M., & Nir, A. R. (2012). The utility of health and wealth. *Journal of Health Economics, 31*(2), 379–392.

Levy, M., & Roll, R. (2016). Seeking alpha? It's a bad guideline for portfolio optimization. *The Journal of Portfolio Management, 42*(5), 107–112.

Levy, M., & Roll, R. (2018). Generalized performance measures: Optimal overweighing of fees relative to sample returns. *The Journal of Portfolio Management, 44*(3), 66–75.

Levy, M., & Roll, R. (2023). The shrinkage adjusted Sharpe ratio: An improved method for mutual fund selection. *The Journal of Investing, 32*(2), 7–23.

Levy, M., & Solomon, S. (1997). New evidence for the power-law distribution of wealth. *Physica a: Statistical Mechanics and Its Applications, 242*(1–2), 90–94.

Lintner, J. (1965). Security prices, risk, and maximal gains from diversification. *The Journal of Finance, 20*(4), 587–615.

Lo, A. W. (2002). The statistics of Sharpe ratios. *Financial Analysts Journal, 58*(4), 36–52.

Lo, A. (2017). *Adaptive markets: Financial evolution at the speed of thought.* Princeton University Press.

Lo, A. W., & MacKinlay, A. C. (2011). *A non-random walk down Wall Street*. Princeton University Press.

Lo, A. W., Orr, H. A., & Zhang, R. (2018). The growth of relative wealth and the Kelly criterion. *Journal of Bioeconomics, 20*, 49–67.

MacLean, L. C., Thorp, E. O., & Ziemba, W. T. (2011). *The Kelly capital growth investment criterion: Theory and practice* (Vol. 3). London: World Scientific.

MacLean, L. C., Ziemba, W. T., & Blazenko, G. (1992). Growth versus security in dynamic investment analysis. *Management Science, 38*(11), 1562–1585.

Malkiel, B. G. (1995). Returns from investing in equity mutual funds 1971 to 1991. *The Journal of Finance, 50*(2), 549–572.

Mandelbrot, B. (1963). The variation of certain speculative prices. *The Journal of Business, 36*(4), 394–419.

Markowitz, H. (1952). Portfolio selection. *The Journal of Finance, 7*(1), 77–91.

Markowitz, H. M. (1976). Investment for the long run: New evidence for an old rule. *The Journal of Finance, 31*(5), 1273–1286.

Markowitz, H. M. (2006). Samuelson and investment for the long run. In M. Szenberg, L. Ramrattan, & A. A. Gottesman (Eds.), *Samuelsonian economics and the twenty-first century* (pp. 252–261). Oxford University Press.

Markowitz, H. (2012). Mean-variance approximations to the geometric mean. *Annals of Financial Economics, 7*(01), 1250001.

Markowitz, H. M., Reid, D. W., & Tew, B. V. (1994). The value of a blank check. *Journal of Portfolio Management, 20*(4), 82.

Mehra, R., & Prescott, E. C. (1985). The equity premium: A puzzle. *Journal of Monetary Economics, 15*(2), 145–161.

Merton, R. C. (1969). Lifetime portfolio selection under uncertainty: The continuous-time case. *The Review of Economics and Statistics, 1969*, 247–257.

Merton, R. C., & Samuelson, P. A. (1974). Fallacy of the log-normal approximation to optimal portfolio decision-making over many periods. *Journal of Financial Economics, 1*(1), 67–94.

Meyer, D. J., & Meyer, J. (2005). Relative risk aversion: What do we know? *Journal of Risk and Uncertainty, 31*, 243–262.

Mossin, J. (1966). Equilibrium in a capital asset market. *Econometrica: Journal of the Econometric Society, 1966*, 768–783.

Mugerman, Y., & Steinberg, N. (2023). *How do mutual fund management fee changes impact mutual fund flows?* Available at SSRN 4603217.

Mullainathan, S., & Shleifer, A. (2005). *Persuasion in finance*. National Bureau of Economic Research (No. w11838).

Newman, H. A., & Mozes, H. A. (1999). Does the composition of the compensation committee influence CEO compensation practices? *Financial Management, 1999*, 41–53.

Oskamp, S. (1965). Overconfidence in case-study judgments. *Journal of Consulting Psychology, 29*(3), 261.

Oyer, P. (2004). Why do firms use incentives that have no incentive effects? *The Journal of Finance, 59*(4), 1619–1650.

Pareto, V. (1897). *Cours d'economique politique* (Vol. 2). Rouge.

Pástor, L., & Stambaugh, R. F. (2002). Mutual fund performance and seemingly unrelated assets. *Journal of Financial Economics, 63*(3), 315–349.

Pástor, L., & Stambaugh, R. F. (2012). On the size of the active management industry. *Journal of Political Economy, 120*(4), 740–781.

Pástor, L., Stambaugh, R. F., & Taylor, L. A. (2015). Scale and skill in active management. *Journal of Financial Economics, 116*(1), 23–45.

Pástor, L., & Vorsatz, M. B. (2020). Mutual fund performance and flows during the COVID-19 crisis. *The Review of Asset Pricing Studies, 10*(4), 791–833.

Persky, J. (1992). Retrospectives: Pareto's law. *Journal of Economic Perspectives, 6*(2), 181–192.

Philips, C. B., & Kinniry Jr, F. M. (2010). *Mutual fund ratings and future performance.* Vanguard Group, 20.

Pool, V. K., Stoffman, N., & Yonker, S. E. (2012). No place like home: Familiarity in mutual fund manager portfolio choice. *The Review of Financial Studies, 25*(8), 2563–2599.

Pool, V. K., Stoffman, N., & Yonker, S. E. (2015). The people in your neighborhood: Social interactions and mutual fund portfolios. *The Journal of Finance, 70*(6), 2679–2732.

Rabin, M. (2002). Inference by believers in the law of small numbers. *The Quarterly Journal of Economics, 117*(3), 775–816.

Rabin, M., & Vayanos, D. (2010). The gambler's and hot-hand fallacies: Theory and applications. *The Review of Economic Studies, 77*(2), 730–778.

Rappaport, A., & Nodine, T. (1999). New thinking on how to link executive pay with performance. *Harvard Business Review, 77*(2), 91–92.

Roll, R. (1973). Evidence on the "growth-optimum" model. *The Journal of Finance, 28*(3), 551–566.

Roll, R. (1977). A critique of the asset pricing theory's tests Part I: On past and potential testability of the theory. *Journal of Financial Economics, 4*(2), 129–176.

Roll, R. (1978). Ambiguity when performance is measured by the securities market line. *The Journal of Finance, 33*(4), 1051–1069.

Roll, R. (1992). A mean/variance analysis of tracking error. *Journal of Portfolio Management, 18*(4), 13.

Roll, R. (1994). What every CFO should know about scientific progress in financial economics: What is known and what remains to be resolved. *Financial Management, 23*(2), 69–75.

Rothschild, M., & Stiglitz, J. (1970). Increasing risk: I. A definition. *Journal of Economic Theory, 2*(3), 225–243.

Samuelson, P. (1969). Lifetime portfolio selection by dynamic stochastic programming. *The Review of Economics and Statistics, 51*(3), 239–246.

Samuelson, P. A. (1989). The judgement of economic science on rational portfolio man. *Journal of Portfolio Management, 16*(1), 4.

Samuelson, P. A. (1994). The long-term case for equities. *Journal of Portfolio Management, 21*(1), 15.

Sharpe, W. F. (1964). Capital asset prices: A theory of market equilibrium under conditions of risk. *The Journal of Finance, 19*(3), 425–442.

Sharpe, W. F. (1966). Mutual fund performance. *The Journal of Business, 39*(1), 119–138.

Sharpe, W. F. (1998). Morningstar's risk-adjusted ratings. *Financial Analysts Journal, 54*(4), 21–33.

Sheng, J., Simutin, M., & Zhang, T. (2023). Cheaper is not better: On the 'superior' performance of high-fee mutual funds. *The Review of Asset Pricing Studies, 13*(2), 375–404.

Siegel, J. J. (2021). *Stocks for the long run: The definitive guide to financial market returns and long-term investment strategies*. McGraw-Hill Education.

Sirri, E. R., & Tufano, P. (1998). Costly search and mutual fund flows. *The Journal of Finance, 53*(5), 1589–1622.

Steindl, J. (1965). *Random processes and the growth of firms: A study of the Pareto law*. Charles Griffin & Company.

Subrahmanyam, A. (2023). *Keeping it simple: The disappearance of premia for standard non-market factors*. https://ssrn.com/abstract=4584638

Surowiecki, J. (2005). *The wisdom of crowds*. Anchor.

Szpiro, G. G. (1986a). Measuring risk aversion: An alternative approach. *The Review of Economics and Statistics, 1986*, 156–159.

Szpiro, G. G. (1986b). Relative risk aversion around the world. *Economics Letters, 20*(1), 19–21.

Szpiro, G. G., & Outreville, J. F. (1988). Relative risk aversion around the world: Further results. *Journal of Banking and Finance, 6*, 127–128.

Takayasu, H. (1990). *Fractals in the physical sciences*. Manchester University Press.

Taleb, N. N. (2016). *Fooled by randomness: The hidden role of chance in life and in the markets*. Editeurs Divers USA.

Tervio, M. (2008). The difference that CEOs make: An assignment model approach. *American Economic Review, 98*(3), 642–668.

Thorp, E. O. (1975). Portfolio choice and the Kelly criterion. In *Stochastic optimization models in finance* (pp. 599–619). Academic Press.

Tobin, J. (1965). The theory of portfolio selection. In F. H. Hahn and F. P. R Brechling (eds.), *The Theory of Interest Rates*, MacMillan, London.

Tully, S. (1998). Raising the bar. *Fortune, 137*, 134–138.

Tversky, A., & Kahneman, D. (1971). Belief in the law of small numbers. *Psychological Bulletin, 76*(2), 105.

Tversky, A., & Kahneman, D. (1973). Availability: A heuristic for judging frequency and probability. *Cognitive Psychology, 5*(2), 207–232.

Tversky, A., & Kahneman, D. (1992). Advances in prospect theory: Cumulative representation of uncertainty. *Journal of Risk and Uncertainty, 5,* 297–323.

Vasicek, O. A. (1973). A note on using cross-sectional information in Bayesian estimation of security betas. *The Journal of Finance, 28*(5), 1233–1239.

Waldfogel, J. (1993). The deadweight loss of Christmas. *The American Economic Review, 83*(5), 1328–1336.

Wang, M. (2023). *Heads I win, tails it's chance: Mutual fund performance self-attribution.* Working paper.

Weiner, B. (1985). An attributional theory of achievement motivation and emotion. *Psychological Review, 92*(4), 548.

Wermers, R. (2000). Mutual fund performance: An empirical decomposition into stock-picking talent, style, transactions costs, and expenses. *The Journal of Finance, 55*(4), 1655–1695.

Wu, C. (2009). Mutual fund advertisements. *Investment Management and Financial Innovations, 6,* 68–76.

Xu, G., & Guerard, J. (2024). Data mining corrections and mutual fund performance. *Journal of Portfolio Management, 2024,* 1.

Young, W. E., & Trent, R. H. (1969). Geometric mean approximations of individual security and portfolio performance. *Journal of Financial and Quantitative Analysis, 4*(2), 179–199.

Zheng, L. (1999). Is money smart? A study of mutual fund investors' fund selection ability. *The Journal of Finance, 54*(3), 901–933.

Zhu, M. (2018). Informative fund size, managerial skill, and investor rationality. *Journal of Financial Economics, 130*(1), 114–134.

Ziemba, W. T. (2015). A response to Professor Paul A. Samuelson's objections to Kelly capital growth investing. *Journal of Portfolio Management, 42*(1), 153.

INDEX

© The Editor(s) (if applicable) and The Author(s), under exclusive license to Springer Nature Switzerland AG 2024
M. Levy and R. Roll, *Mutual Fund Selection*,
https://doi.org/10.1007/978-3-031-69758-6

GPSR Compliance

The European Union's (EU) General Product Safety Regulation (GPSR) is a set of rules that requires consumer products to be safe and our obligations to ensure this.

If you have any concerns about our products, you can contact us on ProductSafety@springernature.com

In case Publisher is established outside the EU, the EU authorized representative is:

Springer Nature Customer Service Center GmbH
Europaplatz 3
69115 Heidelberg, Germany

The manufacturer's authorised representative in the EU is Springer
Nature Customer Service Centre GmbH, Europaplatz 3, 69115 Heidelberg,
Germany. If you have any concerns regarding our products, please
contact ProductSafety@springernature.com

Printed and bound by CPI Group (UK) Ltd, Croydon, CR0 4YY
29/04/2026
02099471-0015